LIFE IN PICTURES

MARILYN
MONROE

LIFE IN PICTURES
MARILYN MONROE

Marie Clayton

Bath · New York · Singapore · Hong Kong · Cologne · Delhi · Melbourne

First published by Parragon in 2010

Parragon
Queen Street House
4 Queen Street
Bath
BA1 1HE

Text © Parragon Books Ltd 2010
For details of photographs see page 256

Produced by Atlantic Publishing

ISBN: 978-1-4454-0582-7

Printed in China

Contents

Introduction

Even many years after her death, Marilyn Monroe is still one of the greatest legends of the twentieth century. In her films she projected a unique and fascinating persona—a child-woman who was both innocent and full of sexuality, someone whom men desired, but who women found unthreatening. In real life, she was a beautiful and complex woman who felt deeply insecure, and who just wanted to be loved enough to wipe out her unhappy past.

She was born on the wrong side of the tracks, an illegitimate and unwanted child, who spent most of her early years in a series of foster homes, and became a teenage bride rather than return to the orphanage. A few years later she discovered the one lover who would never let her down, and started an all-consuming affair with the camera. She fought every adversity and setback with determination and humor, and went on to become the most famous movie star of the twentieth century. In her brief film career she appeared in several classic movies, as well as many more that are memorable simply for her presence.

Life in Pictures: Marilyn Monroe charts Marilyn's fascinating life, from her unhappy childhood, through her time as a superstar, to her tragic early death. The exciting collection of photographs not only includes movie stills and portraits, but also many other less well known pictures taken during her career. The photographs are accompanied by detailed and perceptive captions, which give a rounded portrait of one of the world's greatest movie stars. Marilyn Monroe the person may no longer be with us, but Marilyn Monroe the star is an extraordinary and unforgettable woman whose legend lives on.

CHAPTER ONE

Ladies of the Chorus

After Marilyn Monroe became famous, she told so many different stories about her childhood that it is often not clear where the truth lies. However, she was definitely born on June 1, 1926 in Los Angeles, just a few miles from Hollywood. Her mother, Gladys Pearl, was a film cutter, who worked at Consolidated Film Industries. Gladys had first been married to John Baker, with whom she had two children, Jack and Berniece, but the marriage had ended in divorce in 1923. Afterwards John Baker took the children back to Kentucky, leaving Gladys in California. She wasn't alone for long—in 1924 she met and married Martin Edward Mortensen. This marriage also failed, and Mortensen had long vanished from the scene before Gladys became pregnant with her third child. She never stated who the father was—perhaps she didn't really know—but one of the most likely candidates was Charles Stanley Gifford, foreman of the day shift at Consolidated. Despite this, the new baby was registered as Norma Jeane Mortensen—although during her childhood she was also sometimes known as Norma Jean Baker.

By all accounts, Gladys was not cut out to be a mother. She was still only a teenager when she gave birth to her first two children; she was only just 24 when Norma Jeane was born, and was not in a settled relationship. Gladys had to manage on her own, with only the help of her close friend, Grace McKee. Not long after the birth she had to return to work to support herself, so she arranged for the baby to be cared for by the Bolender family.

Ida Bolender and her husband, Albert Wayne, were a devoutly religious couple who looked after various local children as an extra source of income. Although Marilyn later portrayed herself as being unhappy and living in grinding poverty at this time, there is no evidence that her life was really like that. The Bolenders may not have been rich, but they lived comfortably and Norma Jeane was well dressed, had toys to play with, and was not neglected. She stayed with the Bolenders for seven years—which was the longest period of stability in her childhood. Nevertheless, it was a confusing situation for a young child—she was neither a temporary visitor, nor a part of the family. Ida Bolender had her own son, and there was a procession of other foster children, none of whom stayed as long as Norma Jeane. She later recalled having once called Ida "Mama," and being told that Ida was not her mother—the lady with the red hair was. Her mother came to visit at weekends, although these visits became less frequent as time went by. Marilyn later said that Gladys never seemed to smile, or offer any affection, so she found it difficult to think of her as "mother."

When Norma Jeane was seven Gladys paid the Bolenders to date and took Norma Jeane away with her. She took out a mortgage on a small house in Arbol Street, near the Hollywood Bowl. To finance the payments, she let the house to an English couple with a grown-up daughter, while renting back a room for herself and Norma Jeane to live in. The couple were actors, and their daughter often worked as a stand-in. Since Gladys, and her close friend Grace McKee, were both still working at Consolidated, the talk at home was naturally full of movies and movie stars.

Opposite: Marilyn in *Ladies of the Chorus*.

Unfortunately, this interlude did not last long. Early the following year Gladys was taken to hospital, having suffered a severe bout of depression that swiftly descended into some kind of mental breakdown. She was formally pronounced insane at the end of 1934, and was to spend most of her life in various hospitals until 1967, seemingly having lost her ability to cope with day-to-day life. Meanwhile, the young Norma Jeane was taken in hand by her mother's friend, Grace. Grace had no children of her own and she apparently came to regard the child almost as her own daughter, particularly after she later became Norma Jeane's legal guardian. Grace was a big fan of Jean Harlow, and she began to instill the belief that one day Norma Jeane would also be a famous movie star. She dressed the child up, showed her how to use makeup and took her to the movies regularly. However, her plans were interrupted when she met Erwin "Doc" Goddard, and he and Grace married after a whirlwind courtship. One month later, Norma Jeane entered an orphanage and yet again felt let down, unloved, and abandoned—feelings that were beginning to shape how she would behave and react in the future.

The orphanage was not as bad as she later sometimes painted it, and the studio publicity machine, anxious to take advantage of any opportunity to publicize their new star, also exaggerated its supposed horrors. Grace came to take her for outings at weekends, when they went to the movies or she treated the child to a makeover at the beauty parlor.

When she left the orphanage, soon after her eleventh birthday, Norma Jeane was placed with a series of foster families, before finally going to live with Grace and her husband. Doc had three children from a previous marriage; one of them, Eleanor—known as Beebe—was around the same age as Norma Jeane and the two of them became great friends.

Once more, however, this promised stability was interrupted when Doc was offered a job on the East Coast. Again, Norma Jeane found herself surplus to requirements, as the Goddards decided that they could not afford to take her with them. It also meant that she would lose her first real friend of her own age. However, Grace had a solution—Norma Jean should marry James, the twenty-year-old son of her friend and neighbor, Ethel Dougherty.

Although Norma Jeane and James Dougherty knew each other well, and had even dated on occasion, he was five years older than her and regarded her as still very much a child. But she had a crush on him, and he was flattered by the attention. Grace and Ethel conspired to send them out on regular dates, and soon he came to regard Norma Jeane in a rather different light. However, they probably would not have married—except that for Norma Jeane it was marriage or return to the orphanage, while Jim could see no real reason not to go along with the idea.

After their wedding, the young couple moved into an apartment. Norma Jeane tried hard to be a good wife, but she hated housework and had no idea about cooking. Like many young husbands, Jim saw nothing wrong with seeing his friends regularly, which his wife perceived as a rejection of her company. He found it difficult to cope with her extreme sensitivity and insecurity. When he was posted to Catalina Island, where he trained new recruits, another complication came into play, as Norma Jeane attracted scores of admirers. She had no thought of being unfaithful, but Jim was jealous.

Once Jim was posted abroad, Norma Jeane returned to live with his mother, Ethel, who found her a job at her own workplace, the Radio Plane munitions factory. It was here that army photographer David Conover spotted her, featuring her in many of the shots he took of women doing war work. He was so impressed by her ability to look good on camera that he came back to take more photographs, and suggested that she should try a career as a model. Norma Jeane soon signed up with the Blue Book Agency, based in Sunset Boulevard. The Blue Book not only found modeling assignments, but also ran classes in makeup, grooming, posing, and fashion work and persuaded the new signing to bleach her hair blonde.

As she became successful, Norma Jeane gave up her old job and moved out of her mother-in-law's house and into an apartment. Inevitably Norma Jeane's new life soon led to the end of her marriage to Jim, although they did not officially divorce until September 1946.

Meanwhile, Norma Jeane was introduced to the National Concert Artists Corporation, who became her agents and arranged her first screen test with Twentieth Century Fox in July 1946. Fox offered her a standard six-month contract, with a salary of $75 per week and an option to renew for another six months at twice this. Grace McKee had to sign on Norma Jeane's behalf, as she was still under age. Ben Lyon, head of talent at the studio, also decided that she had to change her name. Norma Jeane wanted to keep the name Jean, and picked Monroe as her surname, after her grandmother. Lyon then suggested her first name should be Marilyn, after stage actress Marilyn Miller. Norma Jeane went along with this—but years later she said she never liked her new name and wished she had held out for Jean.

In her first year under contract she had only three bit parts in B-movies, despite having appeared at hundreds of press calls and photo opportunities. Although Fox had picked up their first option, at the end of the year they declined to renew and Marilyn was out on the Hollywood circuit again, along with thousands of other aspiring starlets. Refusing to give up, she carried on modeling but also cultivated as many movie contacts as possible. At one of countless Hollywood parties she was introduced to Joe Schenck, co-founder of Fox and a very influential ally, who soon persuaded Columbia Studios to hire her on a six-month contract in March 1948. At Columbia, she met drama teacher Natasha Lytess, who took her in hand and later became her personal drama coach, and was given her first proper movie role in *Ladies of the Chorus*. Despite good reviews, this time Marilyn's contract option was not picked up in September.

At this point Marilyn might have despaired, but she soon had a piece of good fortune. At a New Year's Eve Party she met influential agent Johnny Hyde, who was very taken with her and soon invited her out. He not only came to adore Marilyn, but also seemed able to see a star quality in her that others had failed to spot. From this point on, Marilyn's career took a turn for the better. Shortly afterward she had a small but significant part in a Marx Brothers' movie, *Love Happy*, followed by a role as a chorus girl in *A Ticket to Tomahawk*. By August, Johnny was her agent and had turned his full attention to nurturing her career.

A small part in her first high-profile movie, *The Asphalt Jungle* directed by John Huston, began to get her noticed and not long after that she landed a good role in *All About Eve*. This picture was one of the most successful of 1950, and it brought Marilyn to the attention of Fox studio head Darryl Zanuck, and Johnny Hyde was finally able to get her that elusive long-term contract.

Throughout this period, Johnny Hyde had been urging her to marry him—he had left his wife soon after meeting Marilyn and had introduced her to top Hollywood society, as well as paying for minor cosmetic surgery and a wardrobe of good clothes. Not only was he in love with her, he was suffering from heart disease and was worried about what would happen to her after he was gone. If she had married him Marilyn would have been a rich woman, but she consistently refused: partly because she didn't want to marry someone she didn't love, partly because she was still devastated that her voice coach, Fred Karger, had refused to marry her, and finally because she feared she would never be taken seriously as an actress if she was Mrs Johnny Hyde. The decision was to cost her dear—that December, Johnny died suddenly of a heart attack. Marilyn was heartbroken—although she had not loved Johnny, she had cared very deeply for him. His family repossessed everything he had bought her and they threw her out of his home, then after the funeral his associates at the agency refused to take her calls. Marilyn was left in limbo—her contract was coming up for renewal and she had no one to protect her interests.

Once again, she refused to give up and after catching the attention of Spyros Skouras, president of Fox, by attending a dinner in a skin-tight cocktail dress, her contract was renewed. During 1951, Marilyn appeared in several rather insignificant movies for Fox, but in August the studio agreed to loan her to RKO, to film *Clash by Night*, directed by Fritz Lang. This was her first proper dramatic part with a top director, and although her role was just a supporting part she made the most of it, getting some excellent reviews. It was her performance in this movie that finally made Fox sit up and take notice, and decide that perhaps she was ready for a leading role.

A Star is Born...

Opposite: The young Norma Jean Baker was persuaded to join the Blue Book Agency, after photographer David Conover discovered her doing war work in the Radio Plane munitions factory. She was in demand as a model, and it was not long before she was also taken on by National Concert Artists Corporation. A screen test at Fox followed, and a standard six-month contract. It was Ben Lyon at Fox who changed the budding starlet's name to Marilyn Monroe. To create interest in their new starlet, the Fox publicity department concocted a story that Marilyn had been discovered when she had been hired as a babysitter for a casting director and Marilyn was pictured reading a story to three-year-old Joanne Metzler. Stories like these made hundreds of young girls believe that they too could be discovered, if only they were in the right place at the right time.

Right: Another part of the budding starlet's life was a succession of classes, in which she learned acting, singing and dancing, as well as studying movement and voice culture. In contrast to her screen image, in reality Marilyn was no dizzy blonde and worked hard to improve her acting technique, studying at the Actors' Lab off Sunset Boulevard and seeking to perfect every aspect of her performance.

Smile, please...

Opposite: The publicity department took an endless series of "cheesecake" photos of all the Fox contract players. Marilyn was always ready to appear for a photographic session, as she knew her future career depended on being noticed by somebody in a position of power. She was successful in this, first becoming one of Joseph M. Schenck's "girls" and then catching the eye of influential agent Johnny Hyde. Sometimes the publicity pictures took on a more practical aspect, as in this "how to look like a movie-star" beauty session, in which Marilyn is shown applying makeup for the cameras.

Right: A demure-looking Marilyn poses in a strapless gown. At this point in her career she was still one of hundreds of aspiring starlets.

Falling in love

Opposite: In 1948 Marilyn was briefly under contract to Columbia Studios, and had a part in *Ladies of the Chorus*. The movie gave her a chance to sing for the first time, and she was assigned to voice coach Fred Karger. She fell in love with Karger, but he refused to marry her, later marrying actress Jane Wyman instead.

Right: Marilyn gazes lovingly into the eyes of Rand Brooks, who played her handsome socialite boyfriend, Randy Carroll, in the movie. The plot has the two of them planning to marry, despite the social divide which threatens to keep them apart. In the end love conquers all.

Below: Posing for illustrator Earl Moran. Moran was one of America's most renowned cheesecake artists and Marilyn modeled for him regularly between 1946 and 1949, earning $10 an hour. It was steady work that kept her going as she tried to break into the movie business. Moran produced several charcoal and chalk pictures of her that featured on various calendars.

Johnny's girl

Opposite: *Ladies of the Chorus* was shot in only ten days. Marilyn told reporters later that when the movie was released, she was so excited that she drove past the theater several times to see her name on the marquee.

Right: Marilyn poses again. Unfortunately Columbia Studios chief Harry Cohn was not so impressed with her performance in *Ladies of the Chorus* and Marilyn's option was not picked up. However, Marilyn had been taken under the wing of William Morris agent Johnny Hyde, a well-connected Hollywood player who had managed Rita Hayworth. Johnny introduced Marilyn into his social circle and contributed financially to ensure that his protégée looked the part, paying for some minor cosmetic surgery and for hairdressers to color her hair.

Following pages: *Ladies of the Chorus* was Marilyn's first co-starring role. It was only a low-budget "B" movie so it made little impact on her career but it was on the movie that Marilyn met drama coach Natasha Lytess, who became her personal teacher and whose advice and support quickly became indispensable to her insecure pupil.

A ticket to ride...

A *Ticket to Tomahawk* was Marilyn's first movie for Twentieth Century Fox since they had declined to pick up her option two years earlier. In it she played one of four chorus girls in a story that involved a stagecoach owner trying to stop the new-fangled railroad from ruining his business. The movie was a rather low-key musical Western and did little for her career—but it would have done much better if it had been well promoted. Unfortunately, Fox had just released a Betty Grable comic Western, *The Beautiful Blonde from Bashful Bend*, which had been badly reviewed and had done rather poorly, so at the time they were not inclined to spend further money on publicity for another Western that could also prove to be a flop.

The Asphalt Jungle

Opposite: Johnny Hyde was instrumental in getting Marilyn the part of Angela, the mistress of a bent lawyer, in *The Asphalt Jungle*. John Huston's movie was a commericial success but unusual in two ways: it portrayed criminals as ordinary people rather than as gangsters and, more importantly, he had decided not to include any established stars in the cast. Marilyn only had three scenes but she certainly made an impact. Louis Calhern played the lawyer, Alonzo D. Emmerich.

Right: Marilyn with her co-star Dan Dailey in *A Ticket to Tomahawk*.

Below: Anne Baxter, Bette Davis, Marilyn, and George Sanders in a scene from *All About Eve*, which was directed by Joseph L. Mankiewicz. Hyde taught Marilyn that it was better to have a small part in a good movie with an excellent director, than a leading role in a poor movie with a mediocre one. It was this lesson that led to her battle to obtain director and script approval in later years.

Pinup

The editors of *Stars and Stripes*, the newspaper for US occupation forces, voted unanimously to award the title of Miss Cheesecake of 1950 to Marilyn. The 1st Marine Division also christened her Miss Morale as they left for Korea. She always felt that her rise to stardom was accelerated by the devotion of soldiers, for whom she was a favorite pinup.

With a powerful patron behind her and two critically successful movies completed, it seemed that Marilyn was on the way to achieving her ambition. But at the end of 1951 Johnny Hyde died of a heart attack and Marilyn found herself alone and dependent on her own resources again.

Miss Valentine

Opposite: Publicity poses were usually glamour shots, as Fox began to see Marilyn as a replacement for Betty Grable, who was nearing the end of her career. However, Marilyn was still roped in to do her share of opportunistic poses...

Left: For Valentine's Day 1951, she was dressed in a sexy two-piece cowgirl costume and posed with a heart-shaped target.

Above: Although Marilyn only had a small part in *As Young As You Feel*, her name was billed above the title to capitalize on her recent success. It had also convinced studio head Darryl Zanuck to finally offer her a long-term contract. In a scene from the movie, Marilyn, as Harriet, takes dictation from industry boss Louis McKinley, played by Albert Dekker. It was on the set of *As Young As You Feel*, while she was still grieving over the death of Johnny Hyde, that Elia Kazan introduced Marilyn to the playwright Arthur Miller—an encounter that Marilyn did not forget.

Gentlemen Prefer Blondes

Although at the end of 1951 Fox did try Marilyn as the lead in a serious drama—*Don't Bother to Knock*—it was not very successful commercially and she was soon back in light comedy roles. The first of these was *Monkey Business*, a screwball comedy in which Marilyn played the only sane character. When it was released, it was a measure of her growing popularity that theater owners often featured her name to publicize the movie, rather than those of her more famous co-stars, Cary Grant and Ginger Rogers.

Whenever Marilyn worked, her personal drama coach, Natasha Lytess, had to be near by on the set. Marilyn originally met Natasha at Columbia, where she had been the drama coach assigned to help the young starlet prepare for her role in *Ladies of the Chorus*. When Marilyn had signed her new contract with Fox, the only privilege she had asked for was that Natasha should be hired as her personal drama coach, and to work with other contract players when possible. Marilyn's reliance on Natasha often drove her directors and co-stars mad. Rather than looking to the director at the end of a take, she sought Natasha's approval—and if she didn't get it she would ask for a retake. Directors resented a second authority usurping their own, while other actors were put under pressure, as they knew that the take used would be the best one of Marilyn, so they had to be good every time.

While Marilyn was working on *Monkey Business*, a potential disaster loomed. In May 1949, she had posed nude for photographer Tom Kelley, and the picture had been used anonymously on a 1952 calendar—which now adorned gas stations and barbershops across the country. Someone had recognized Marilyn as the blonde stretched out artistically on red velvet, and the story was about to break in the press. In the moral climate of the early 1950s, the scandal could have ruined her budding career—posing nude was not something a nice girl did, and no Hollywood star had ever been caught out behaving in such a way. Fox executives were all for denying the whole thing, but Marilyn thought she should just tell the truth and admit everything—and for the first time, her view prevailed. An exclusive interview was arranged with journalist Aline Mosby, and the story ran in US newspapers in March. Marilyn confessed that she was the blonde, and explained that she had desperately needed the money to pay off debts and that this had been the only honest way she could earn it quickly. She mentioned that the photographer's wife had been present at the shoot, and said that she felt she had done nothing to be ashamed of. The result was a triumph, instead of a disaster. Public sympathy swung behind her and the calendar was reprinted many times during the early fifties—it is estimated that as many as four million copies were sold.

Two days after the story broke, Marilyn met baseball star Joe DiMaggio for the first time. He had seen a publicity photograph of her with two White Sox players, and asked who she was. Later he discovered that one of his drinking

Opposite: Marilyn shows off some of her assets.

buddies knew her and could arrange an introduction. After dinner he called her every night and they were soon a famous couple, with their romance documented in all the newspapers. Marilyn loved the warmth of his Italian family and valued the feeling of security he gave her, and the impression that he was batting on her side.

She certainly needed support, as within a couple of months another potential threat to her career appeared. All the publicity about Marilyn as she became a star had been built around the fact that she was an orphan, who had become successful despite adversity. Now a journalist had tracked down her mother—who was not only still alive, but had just been released from the latest in a series of state mental institutions. Coming just after the "nude calendar revelations," the timing could not have been worse. Marilyn quickly gave another exclusive interview, this time to Erskine Johnson, saying that she had not known as a child, when she had spent time in an orphanage and in foster homes, that her mother was in hospital. She also said that, having discovered that her mother was still alive, she had been in contact and was offering help as required. The last part at least was true—Marilyn's business manager, Inez Melson, had been visiting Gladys to make sure she had sufficient money since 1951. Again, the explanation was accepted and Marilyn retained her public following.

Meanwhile, she was about to begin work on her next major starring role. In Niagara, she played a sultry seductress who plans to murder her husband so she can be with her lover. The scene where Marilyn croons along with a record was so sexually charged that it outraged representatives from the Women's Clubs of America, and had to be hastily modified. Throughout filming, Marilyn pushed the limits of what was acceptable, and she outshone the more experienced actors with whom she was working. When she was on the screen, the audience didn't look at anyone else. After the movie was completed, everyone was left in no doubt that Marilyn was truly a star.

In 1952, five movies featuring Marilyn were released —Clash by Night for RKO and We're Not Married, Don't Bother to Knock, Monkey Business, and O Henry's Full House for Fox. Her next picture for Fox was already lined up. The studio had originally bought the rights to Gentlemen Prefer Blondes for Betty Grable, but director Howard Hawks, who had recently worked with Marilyn on Monkey Business, was convinced she was perfect for the part of Lorelei Lee. Despite some studio reservations as to whether she was up to the demands of the role, she was paired with Jane Russell and at the beginning of November 1952 work started on costume and makeup tests. In this movie, Marilyn has a far more sophisticated look than she had achieved before—and this is often attributed to the influence of Hawks. For the dance numbers, Marilyn worked hard with choreographer Jack Cole to perfect her technique, because she knew she had no natural ability here, as she did with acting and singing.

By now, Marilyn was beginning to cause problems on set with her chronic lateness. She would arrive at the studio early, but was still locked in her dressing room hours after filming was due to start. It was a habit that often drove her directors and co-workers crazy, because they saw it as evidence of unprofessionalism or laziness or as deliberate rudeness. However, on this movie co-star Jane Russell soon realized the cause. It wasn't that Marilyn would not come to the set—she couldn't. She was terrified of going in front of the camera, because she could not bear the thought of failing, of being less than perfect. She spent hours doing and re-doing her makeup, and working herself up to the point at which she could perform. It was this very intensity with which she approached her roles that came over on the screen, and made her such a unique star. Jane provided a simple and fairly effective solution—every morning she would stop by Marilyn's dressing room and collect her. Once on set, Marilyn would work, as long as the atmosphere was conducive, and as long as Natasha was on hand.

The following year, 1953, was one of the high points in Marilyn's career. In January, Niagara was released and went on to earn more than five times what it had cost to make, confirming Marilyn as a top box-office draw. In April she began work on another major role, co-starring in How to Marry a Millionaire. In this, she was working with two well-established stars, Betty Grable and Lauren Bacall. The studio made much of a supposed feud between Marilyn and Betty—the incoming star and the outgoing one—but in fact they got on well and became great friends. Although she had been dubious about playing the part of a girl who wore glasses, the "accidents" built round her character's nearsightedness confirmed Marilyn's talent as an actress with a gift for comedy.

In July, *Gentlemen Prefer Blondes* was released, and it quickly became a spectacular success. Both the public and the critics loved it and it brought Marilyn her first award for her talent, rather than her looks—*Photoplay* magazine's Best Actress of 1953.

Marilyn had gone straight from *Gentlemen Prefer Blondes* to *How to Marry a Millionaire*, with little rest in between, and now she was about to start on *River of No Return*. Charles Feldman of Famous Artists, who was acting as her agent although she had not signed the contract, was becoming concerned about the effect of continuous working on her health—and was worried that her career might be damaged by overexposure. When the studio informed her that immediately after *River of No Return* they intended to put her in another musical, *The Girl in Pink Tights*, Feldman advised her to turn the project down. He also thought that this would signal to studio executives that he and Marilyn were aware of just how important she had become, as a prelude to renegotiating her contract. On the one hand Marilyn was reluctant to turn down an assignment because of her insecurity, and because she had no savings to tide her over if the studio suspended her, but on the other she had her own worries about accepting the movie. Firstly, she was annoyed that no one thought it important that she should see the script—she had only been sent a précis of the plot—and from that, it was evident that the character was similar to those she had played in her last two pictures. This fuelled another worry—she was afraid of being typecast and outliving her usefulness, so she wanted to play a wider range of roles. In addition to the studio choosing all her projects with no reference to her, they were also assigning the director, and Marilyn had learned how important it was to work with directors who could bring out the best in her. Lastly, yet again she was being expected to star in a movie for her usual salary of $1,500 a week—negotiated way back in 1951 before she had become a star—while her co-star, Frank Sinatra, would be paid $5,000 a week. She went off to

Canada for location filming on *River of No Return* with these issues still unresolved.

Marilyn had another problem to sort out. Joe DiMaggio had several times asked her to marry him, but she couldn't make up her mind what to do. She loved him and valued the stability and support he offered—but he was not interested in art and books, as she was, and was incredibly jealous of any attention she received from other men. Most of their arguments were to do with her need for public adulation and her habit of dressing provocatively. More importantly, he wanted her to give up the movies and become a beautiful, ex-movie-star housewife, while she was still focused on obtaining the respect and adulation in her career that she felt she deserved. They decided that Joe should join her in Canada, and away from the stresses of Hollywood they would try to come to a decision.

The filming of *River of No Return* was not a happy experience for many of those concerned. Director Otto Preminger made little secret of his lack of enthusiasm for the project and took a great dislike to Natasha Lytess. When Natasha upset child actor Tommy Rettig, causing him to forget his lines, Preminger banned her from the set, but Marilyn quietly made sure that the studio reinstated her. Both Marilyn and co-star Robert Mitchum had physically demanding roles, and part of the plot involved traveling down rapids on a raft, which meant that they had to spend a great deal of time doused in water for continuity.

After filming finished, Joe took Marilyn off to spend a few days with his family in San Francisco, and then they returned to Hollywood. Although he wanted her to give up the movies, he could understand her battles with the studio—particularly over money. Money meant respect—so the more money they were prepared to pay, the more they respected you. On the matter of *The Girl in Pink Tights*, Marilyn was now ready to give in and start work on the movie. However, at this point DiMaggio proved what an astute businessman he was, by pointing out that if Marilyn refused the movie, Fox would have no backlog of Monroe pictures to release, thus putting Feldman in a much stronger bargaining position. When the first day of shooting arrived, Marilyn failed to turn up on set.

We're Not Married

Above: Actor David Wayne looks stony-faced as Marilyn gives him a peck on the cheek in a scene from *We're Not Married* which had a star-studded cast including Ginger Rogers, Fred Allen, and Zsa Zsa Gabor. Marilyn plays a housewife who enters the Mrs America beauty pageant. Her role was hastily added to the story line to cash in on her growing popularity, and scriptwriter Nunnally Johnson later admitted he had deliberately created opportunities for her to appear in two swimsuits.

Opposite: Although the studio had begun to cast her in a steady stream of pictures, Marilyn had not forgotten the importance of publicity and was still prepared to pose for photographers. It would not be long though before she yearned to escape from the "blonde bombshell" image.

Right: Marilyn poses with actor Keith Andes, who played her love-interest in *Clash by Night*, which was released in 1952. She had been loaned out by Fox to RKO and it was her first major role in which some serious acting was required. She insisted that her personal drama coach, Natasha Lytess, was present on set, which did not please director Fritz Lang, although eventually a compromise was reached.

Dating Joe DiMaggio

Above: Marilyn and Joe DiMaggio met on a date in March 1952 at the Villa Nova restaurant and soon became an item. When Joe DiMaggio visited the set of Marilyn's new movie, *Monkey Business*, he was photographed with Cary Grant and Marilyn—but newspaper editors cropped out Cary Grant and photographs of Joe and Marilyn were sent around the world.

Opposite: Marilyn checks out her appearance. Later she would spend hours in front of the mirror before appearing on set—not because she was vain, but because she couldn't bring herself to appear until she thought everything was absolutely perfect.

A little monkey business...

Right: Marilyn appears in a swimsuit in publicity stills for *Monkey Business*. The movie was a screwball comedy starring Cary Grant and Ginger Rogers but shortly before shooting began studio boss Darryl Zanuck asked the scriptwriters to expand both Marilyn's part and that of the monkey!

While she was filming *Monkey Business*, Marilyn developed appendicitis but she refused to go into hospital for an operation until the end of April after she had completed her part. However, although she was prepared to put up with a lot of pain in order to retain her part in the movie, she was reputedly regularly late arriving on set, a habit that was to become more pronounced in the years to come. Howard Hawks later said of her that she was "late every day... but she knew all her lines."

Opposite: Marilyn signs an autograph for a fan. Later a group of New York-based fans were known as the Monroe Six, and they were always present when she was due to appear. When she lived in New York they followed her around, tipping each other off as to what she was doing. She valued their devotion, and once invited all of them to a picnic at Roxbury, where she was living with Arthur Miller.

Calm before a storm

Left: Marilyn relaxes in the sun on the terrace of her home in Hollywood. However, just as she had finally realized her childhood ambitions, Marilyn was recognized as the nude model in a calendar which had been distributed all over the US and the morality clause in her contract allowed the studio to dismiss her should the public react unfavorably to this revelation. However, in contrast to the advice of the studio publicists, Marilyn's instinct was to admit that she had modeled for the pictures, pleading poverty as the motive. The public forgave her and the publicity only increased her profile.

Niagara Falls

Above: Marilyn with Henry Hathaway, director of *Niagara*. In her second leading role, Marilyn shared star billing only with Niagara Falls. The movie featured what was the longest walk in screen history at the time 116 feet of Marilyn swiveling her hips provocatively as she moved away from the camera, wearing a tight black skirt. It caused a sensation—but Marilyn told readers of *Life* magazine, "I've been walking since I was six months old—I just use it to get me around."

Opposite: A publicity picture. From the start of her career Marilyn was thought of by many as just a dumb blonde. It was a stereotype that infuriated her, as it prevented her being considered for more serious acting roles. Part of this was due to studio head Darryl Zanuck, who considered Marilyn to be "empty-headed," but it is debatable whether Marilyn would have risen so high so fast if her early screen roles had been more varied. As it was, she quickly developed a persona that the public loved—and then spent the rest of her career trying to get away from it.

Gentlemen Prefer Blondes

Above: Marilyn arrives in New York in October 1952 to publicize *Monkey Business*. However, this would be one of the few public appearances she would make for some months. After years of tirelessly seeking publicity to advance her career, the studio signaled a new confidence in her and Marilyn was instructed to concentrate solely on preparing for her new role in Howard Hawks's latest project, *Gentlemen Prefer Blondes*, based on the book by Anita Loos.

A birthday present

Having already directed Marilyn in *Monkey Business*, Howard Hawks understood that comedy, rather than drama, was her forte. He persuaded Darryl Zanuck, head of production at Fox, that the combination of established Jane Russell and popular new-comer Marilyn Monroe could be successful at the box office. On her 26th birthday Marilyn was thrilled to be offered the part of Lorelei, created on Broadway by Carol Channing.

Above: Marilyn's drama coach Natasha Lytess explains a point between takes.

Right: Jane Russell with Marilyn on the set of *Gentlemen Prefer Blondes*. The two stars got on very well together— even though Russell was being paid ten times what Marilyn earned for making the movie under her standard studio contract.

Two little girls from Little Rock...

Opposite: Jane and Marilyn play two showgirls traveling to France on a cruise liner, where Lorelei is to marry her wealthy boyfriend, Gus Esmond. Esmond Sr is convinced Lorelei is a gold digger, and hires a private detective to prove it. Marilyn was determined not to squander the opportunity offered to her. She worked late into the evenings to perfect Jack Cole's dance routines. Together the girls performed the show's opening number "Two Little Girls from Little Rock" but the best-remembered song in the movie is Marilyn's rendition of "Diamonds Are a Girl's Best Friend."

Above: After seeing a diamond tiara belonging to Lady Beekman, Lorelei tries out a napkin ring for effect, commenting that she loves to find new places to wear diamonds.

Left: Newcomer Tommy Noonan played the wealthy playboy, Gus Esmond. His rather naive character stood little chance against the wiles of blonde bombshell Lorelei.

A strong support team

Above: Irene Crosby, Marilyn's stand-in on *Gentlemen Prefer Blondes*, poses with the star. On set Marilyn had gathered round her a small group of people with whom she had a strong rapport. Natasha was always present, but loyal makeup man Whitey Snyder and hairdresser Gladys Whitten were also there to encourage and support her.

Opposite: Marilyn studies some of theater-director Max Reinhardt's original manuscripts, which she had recently acquired at auction, paying $1,335. Her interest in the papers no doubt stemmed from the fact that Natasha Lytess had been part of Reinhardt's theater company in Germany. Marilyn's purchase caused the press to complain that she had deprived a university library of the chance to have the manuscripts, which would have meant they were available for all students to study. Marilyn replied that she was thinking of donating them. However, Reinhardt's son acquired them from her at cost and then sold them on at a handsome profit.

On the chalkboard:
```
HAWKS A 698
MARILYN MONROE
AS "LORELEI"
# 10
NT SHIPS CORRIDOR
44, 45
NT MALONES CABIN 4697
ON BOAT DECK-48
ON TELEPHONE-50
# 11
NT LORELEIS LIVING
```

Dressed to impress...

Opposite and above: Leading Hollywood costume designer William Travilla—known simply as Travilla—designed many of the dresses that Marilyn wore in her movies, including the outfits for *Gentlemen Prefer Blondes*. But both Howard Hawks and Travilla could take credit for the slick and sophisticated costumes in the picture which helped change Marilyn's image on screen.

Following pages: Marilyn and Jane Russell were invited to leave their prints outside Grauman's Chinese Theater as part of the publicity for the release of *Gentlemen Prefer Blondes*. Marilyn jokingly suggested that they should leave imprints of what they were famous for instead—her behind and Russell's chest.

More clouds on the horizon

Opposite: Marilyn looks competely in control in this publicity picture. However, no sooner had she dealt with the crisis over the calendar photographs than her mother came back to haunt her—the publicity office at Fox had told the press that Marilyn was an orphan, but a persistent reporter tracked Gladys Baker down and found out she had recently been released from a state mental hospital.

Above: Gossip columnist Walter Winchell, Marilyn, and Joe Schenck at a party for Winchell's birthday at Ciro's in Hollywood in May 1953. Winchell was also a friend of Joe DiMaggio.

Right: According to movie cameraman Frank Powolny, Marilyn had the best rear view of all the movie stars he had photographed during his career.

How to Marry a Millionaire

Marilyn as Pola Debevoise in *How to Marry a Millionaire*, with co-stars Betty Grable (center) and Lauren Bacall (right). The movie was designed to capitalize on the success of *Gentlemen Prefer Blondes*. At the start of production Marilyn was already exhausted by having expended so much energy in mastering the routines on her previous picture and was further handicapped by her usual nerves in front of the camera.

On the Jack Benny Show

Opposite: Marilyn's character was terribly nearsighted but refused to wear her glasses in public, which led to a lot of comic mishaps.

Above: Marilyn gets a hug from comedian Jack Benny in a publicity picture for her guest appearance on his show, transmitted live from the Shrine Auditorium in Los Angeles on September 13, 1953. Marilyn performed a comedy skit with Benny and sang "Bye Bye Baby" before taking the opportunity to mention the release of *How to Marry a Millionaire*. She was thought to have aquitted herself well playing opposite the very experienced Jack Benny and despite the fact that she frequently needed multiple takes when acting in movies, she did not seem unduly worried that the program was live.

River of No Return

Opposite: During the filming of *River of No Return* in Alberta, Canada, in August 1953, Marilyn slipped on some wet rocks and injured her leg. It had to be bandaged and she was forced to hobble around for several days. This was not the only difficulty on set. During the filming of *How to Marry a Millionaire*, director Jean Negulesco had sought to accommodate Marilyn's wishes by tolerating Natasha Lytess's interference. However, on *River of No Return*, Otto Preminger banned Natasha from the set, insisting that she remain in Marilyn's dressing room. The movie over-ran and Marilyn's co-star Robert Mitchum is said to have dubbed it "the picture of no return."

Below: Yet another swimsuit pose... All the photographers that Marilyn worked with commented on how professional and dedicated she was.

Left: Trying on different outfits before posing for a photograph to promote safety during the forthcoming Independence Day celebrations.

Still undecided

Above: Joe and Marilyn continued to date although he preferred to stay out of the limelight. He seldom accompanied her on public appearances, sometimes waiting outside to collect her at the end of the evening. Joe joined Marilyn in Canada while she was filming *River of No Return*. They had been dating for more than a year, but Marilyn could not make up her mind whether to marry him.

Opposite: Tommy Rettig, who appeared in *River of No Return*, and Marilyn attending a movie. After a shaky start the two of them got on well together.

There's No Business Like Show Business

Fox's response to Marilyn's failure to start on *The Girl in Pink Tights* was immediate. They couldn't get hold of Marilyn herself, who was lying low protected by Joe, but they contacted both her agents and Natasha. Famous Artists informed the studio that she was not ready to start on the movie because she still hadn't seen the script. Marilyn had trusted Natasha to be on her side, come what may, but in this instance—perhaps worried about losing her lucrative job—Natasha criticized Marilyn's behavior and tried to get her to relent. Marilyn never forgave her for it, and although they worked together on two more pictures, from then on Natasha's days were numbered.

Meanwhile the studio asked Marilyn to report in, to shoot retakes on *River of No Return*. Everyone understood that it was one thing to refuse to start a project, and quite another to fail to finish one, thus preventing its release and costing the studio hundreds of thousands of dollars. Marilyn's first instinct was that it was a ruse to get her onto the lot, so she fled to San Francisco with Joe. However, her agents discovered that the retakes were indeed necessary, and persuaded her to return. As soon as they were completed, Marilyn returned to San Francisco and continued to sit tight. The studio had no option but to suspend her.

But there was an unexpected twist to come. Marilyn appreciated everything Joe was doing for her—far from holding himself aloof from the movie business as he had done before, now he was fully involved in sorting out her problems with the executives at Fox. Perhaps she took this to mean that he was reconciled to her continuing her career,

and she finally agreed to be his wife. They were married in San Francisco, and only on the day did Marilyn call the studio to let them know. Despite efforts to keep the wedding quiet, the press turned up in force and pictures appeared in all the newspapers. Fox had little option but to lift the suspension—to do otherwise would have seemed churlish—and they informed Famous Artists that Marilyn should report to work at the end of January, after the honeymoon.

For more than a week, the newlyweds enjoyed the seclusion of a remote cabin in the mountains. Marilyn said later that it was during this period that she and Joe really got to know one another. However, at the end of January Joe had to be in New York, so they returned to Los Angeles—to find that Fox had finally sent a copy of the script for *The Girl in Pink Tights*. After reading it, Marilyn still did not want to do the movie. She was put back on suspension and the studio released a press statement pointing out that her last few movies had been outstandingly successful, which was all the evidence needed that they were the best people to decide what she should work on. In the background to this public furore, Charles Feldman of Famous Artists was quietly renegotiating Marilyn's contract. She wanted more money, and approval of the script, director and cinematographer.

Since she was back on suspension again Marilyn was a free agent, so Joe invited her to come with him to Japan as a continuation of their honeymoon. They were going to Tokyo for the opening of the baseball season, but when they arrived it was Marilyn, not Joe, who was the center

Opposite: Marilyn and Joe on their wedding day.

of attention. At a press conference in their hotel, all the questions were directed at her and she announced that she planned to spend a few days in Korea, entertaining US soldiers. Joe did not approve, but Marilyn had always been a big favorite with the troops and felt she owed much of her early success to their support.

Back in Los Angeles, Marilyn found out that Fox had agreed to drop *The Girl in Pink Tights* and instead offered her a role in *There's No Business Like Show Business*, with the promise of the lead in *The Seven Year Itch*—a successful Broadway play to be directed by Billy Wilder. She was back on salary, but only until August 1954, when a new contract would come into force, giving her an additional fee of $100,000 for *The Seven Year Itch*. However, the studio refused to budge on her last requirement. It was always unlikely that they would—at Fox, Zanuck alone decided what movies were going to be made and who was going to make them. If he gave in to Marilyn, who knows what concessions others would demand in future? Marilyn scaled down her demands, asking only for approval of her choreographer and dramatic coach, but the studio would not agree to this either. Finally, however, they conceded that Marilyn should be consulted about the choice of coach and choreographer. It seemed as if matters were settled—but now Marilyn knew that she would not get the creative control she wanted, she was already working on other plans.

Marilyn's character in *There's No Business Like Show Business* was hastily tacked on at the last minute, to create an alternative project she could work on instead of *The Girl in Pink Tights*. The result was not entirely successful, but the main function of the storyline was to provide a framework for the songs of Irving Berlin and the cast included established stars like Ethel Merman and singer Johnnie Ray. Marilyn worked hard on her routines, so as not to be outclassed by her more experienced song-and-dance co-stars. Unfortunately she didn't get on with the director, Walter Lang, and was suffering from the after-effects of a bout of pneumonia, caught entertaining the troops in Korea in below-freezing temperatures. Most critics agree that it is one of her less successful movies, and Marilyn was deeply upset at its lukewarm reception. She felt she had caved in to studio assertions that they knew what was best for her, and now she was being panned for it.

Since the schedule on *There's No Business Like Show Business* had overrun, Marilyn was forced to start *The Seven Year Itch* with no break in between. When she left for location filming in New York, Joe put on a good show when seeing her off at the airport, but in fact their marriage was already in trouble. Joe's jealousy had boiled over on more than one occasion—perhaps even into physical violence, according to some reports—and Marilyn was beginning to feel that she had made a big mistake. However, Joe did still love her and a few days later he followed her to New York. Generally he kept out of the way when she was working, but on one occasion he was on hand for the shooting of the famous skirt scene in *The Seven Year Itch*. As Marilyn stood over the subway grating, with her skirt blowing up almost to her waist and thousands of New Yorkers cheering and yelling, he was seen leaving the street with a grim expression on his face. When Marilyn came back to the hotel they had a furious row, and by the next morning their marriage was all but over.

Although her private life now lay in tatters, at least her professional life was coming together. In 1953, photographer Milton Greene had taken a series of pictures of her that she loved, and which unfortunately seemed to capture a different Marilyn, bringing out aspects of her personality that no one else seemed to see. Since then Greene had listened to her complaints about the studio and, keen to break into film production himself, he had suggested they form their own production company. As soon as it became obvious that Marilyn was not to get the creative control she wanted from Fox, she started talking seriously to Milton Greene about forming Marilyn Monroe Productions. With her own company she would be able to choose her roles and would have the control over her career that she so desperately wanted. She also planned to dispense with Famous Artists as her agents and move over to MCA, as she felt Feldman had failed to achieve even the most basic improvements to her contract.

In December 1954, Marilyn moved to New York, first staying in a hotel and then moving in with Greene and his wife at their house in Weston, Connecticut. Early the following year, Marilyn and Milton Greene held a press conference to announce the formation of Marilyn Monroe Productions. Fox were not going to give up its biggest star without a fight, and their legal representatives quickly pointed out that Marilyn was under exclusive contract to them for the next four years. However, lawyers for Marilyn Monroe Productions had studied the contracts with Fox, and found a number of anomalies and broken promises—including non-payment of the $100,000 additional fee for *The Seven Year Itch*—which they ruled meant the contract was null and void.

The legal battles were to continue throughout 1955, although halfway through the year the emphasis changed. Marilyn Monroe Productions had planned to find a financial backer to enable them to develop their own projects, but as time went by it became apparent that this was not going to happen—and meanwhile Marilyn had a lifestyle to maintain. At first, Fox had *The Seven Year Itch* in the can ready to release, but after it proved astoundingly successful they had no more Monroe movies to follow it up with. At the end of December 1955, Marilyn and Fox signed a new contract, which not only gave her a much more lucrative financial deal—including a percentage of the profits—but also the creative controls she craved, with approval of script, director, and cinematographer. In addition, she was permitted to undertake one independent film project each year. At the time it was an unprecedented amount of power for an actor to have, and represented the first breach in the traditional studio system.

Marilyn made no movies throughout the whole of 1955—concentrating instead on developing her acting skills by working with Lee Strasberg at his Actors Studio. Strasberg believed that she had great talent and he was a major influence on her future acting style. At first she was too insecure to go to the general sessions at the Actors Studio, so he taught her privately at his home. He also advised her to begin psychoanalysis to release the unresolved tensions from her childhood, and Marilyn rushed to follow his instructions, starting sessions with Dr Margaret Hohenberg. Lee Strasberg also went on to provide the replacement for Natasha, in the form of his wife, Paula, who took over the role of personal drama coach on Marilyn's remaining movies.

In New York, Marilyn was able to move around incognito when she wished, by the simple expedient of wearing casual clothes, covering her hair, and wearing dark glasses. Most of the time she found this liberating, but sometimes she couldn't resist slipping back into the Marilyn persona. Several people who witnessed the transformation were fascinated by it. At one moment she would seem like an ordinary person, hardly worthy of a second glance, and then she seemed to throw some kind of inner switch and a magnetism suddenly appeared, turning heads and causing people to flock round her.

During this time, Marilyn also became a part of New York literary life in a way she had never been in Hollywood, introduced to exclusive circles by the Greenes. She appeared at parties and first nights, and also donated her services to charity on several occasions. Despite the fact that their divorce was about to be finalized, Joe DiMaggio was also still very much on the scene: he turned up regularly in New York to take Marilyn out or to offer help and support. Reporters sometimes took this as a sign of an imminent reconciliation, but Marilyn always denied that they were anything more than just friends. Joe might have wished for more, but Marilyn in fact had already quietly begun a relationship with playwright Arthur Miller.

She and Arthur Miller had first met in Hollywood back in 1950, and after he returned to New York she had written to him several times. Miller was one of the most celebrated playwrights of the day, and had won the Pulitzer Prize for his 1948 play, *Death of a Salesman*, although he had struggled to repeat its success subsequently. Now Marilyn was living in New York and moving in literary circles, it was only a matter of time before they would meet again. Miller had been attracted to Marilyn from the first, as she was to him, but he was married, with two young children. He didn't want to divorce his wife, and she didn't want to be a home-wrecker, so nothing further had come of it. Now, however, Miller's marriage was in trouble anyway. As they spent more and more time together—both in private and in public—the press soon got wind of their unlikely friendship. At the first night of Miller's play *A View from the Bridge*, Marilyn met his parents for the first time. Not long afterwards, she was invited to their home, and after she left Miller told them that she was the girl he was going to marry.

Tying the knot

Above and opposite below: At the time of her wedding Marilyn was in dispute and on suspension from Fox, but she called the studio publicists an hour before the wedding to let them know. It was long enough for them to put the word round and—despite the happy couple's desire to keep the ceremony private—hundreds of reporters descended on San Francisco town hall after having been tipped off. The press were excluded from the actual ceremony, but afterwards Joe and Marilyn smiled for photographers and waved to the fans as they hurried to Joe's blue Cadillac. They spent their honeymoon night at the Clifton Motel in Paso Robles, before vanishing to a hideway cabin in the mountains to spend some tranquil time walking in the woods and fishing.

Love birds

Right: Although it had taken some time to come to a decision, there is no doubting the genuine feelings between Marilyn and Joe as they snuggle up to each other in the judge's chambers on their wedding day in January 1954. The wedding itself was planned as a rather low-key affair; Marilyn wore a neat chocolate-brown suit with an ermine collar and Joe a dark blue suit with the same polka dot tie he had worn on his first date with Marilyn. Joe had wanted to marry in a church, but both he and Marilyn were divorced so it was not possible. During the brief, three-minute ceremony, Marilyn promised to "love, honor, and cherish" her husband—but the word "obey" was left out.

En route to Tokyo

Opposite: Joe had been invited to Tokyo to open the 1954 Japanese baseball season, and since she was back on suspension after refusing to appear in *The Girl in Pink Tights*, Marilyn decided to accompany him. Here they are pictured during a brief stopover in Honolulu. Throughout the trip it was Marilyn who was the center of attention. So soon after their honeymoon, the trip had brought home to Joe how difficult it would be to be married to the world's greatest sex-symbol. He was not comfortable with his wife being admired by other men, and more crucially he disliked the fact that Marilyn encouraged them and enjoyed all the attention.

Above: Marilyn arrives at Seoul City Airport by chopper, on her way to entertain the American troops who were still stationed in war-torn Korea. She had been invited by the Far East command of General John E. Hull.

In Korea

Opposite: Despite the sub-zero temperatures and occasional flurries of snow, Marilyn appeared in a low-cut, skin-tight purple sequined gown—with no underwear. At the time she did not appear to notice the cold but she was to suffer for it later, coming down with pneumonia after she had returned to Japan. Here her famous wiggle is demonstrated to appreciative troops, who answered with whistles, cat calls, and applause.

Above: Sergeant Guy Morgan, from Marion, North Carolina, presents Marilyn with a 25th Division "Wolfhounds" scarf.

Right: During the four-day tour, Marilyn did ten shows, singing such favorites as "Diamonds Are a Girl's Best Friend," "Bye Bye Baby," and "Somebody to Love Me." She also included "Do It Again," but the lyrics had to be toned down to "kiss me again" to avoid inflaming the over-excited audience any further. Here she is on stage at the K-47 airbase in Chunchon, Korea.

A rapturous welcome

Left: Many of the soldiers who had come to see Marilyn had walked for over ten miles and they gave her a rapturous welcome. While she was in Korea, many of her performances were filmed and the footage was later put together to create a documentary, which she narrated.

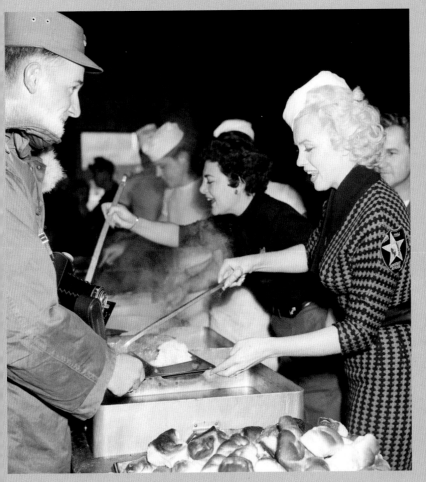

Helping out

Above: Private First Class James R. Goggin gets a bit of personal service, as Marilyn helps out in the 2nd Division Mess.

Opposite below: Marilyn samples the food herself. Later soldiers said that her appetite was "Great, she eats everything."

No Joe...

At the *Photoplay* magazine awards in Hollywood in March 1954, Marilyn was pictured with actor Alan Ladd (above). She explained to the press that Joe did not like crowds—but he came to collect her afterwards. Marilyn had been honored as Most Popular Film Actress of 1953.

Having spent some time with Joe in San Francisco, Marilyn was still under suspension, but had returned to Hollywood for the *Photoplay* awards. The contractual negotiations between the studio and Charles Feldman were protracted but sufficient progress had been made for her to begin work on *There's No Business Like Show Business*. *The Girl in Pink Tights* had been dropped and Fox conceded that Marilyn should not make more than two movies each year. However, she had been refused the level of creative control she sought, only being granted approval of the choreographer and dramatic coach.

Starting a family?

Opposite: Marilyn in her dressing room. Due to her lingering illness throughout filming, Marilyn apparently fainted three times on set, which gave rise to rumors that she was pregnant. She told interested newsmen that she and Joe certainly wanted to start a family, but that she was not yet expecting.

Above: Marilyn demonstrates her singing and dancing skills in *There's No Business Like Show Business*. Her part had been written into the script specially, to give her an alternative project to *The Girl in Pink Tights*.

Left: Marilyn with co-star Johnnie Ray, who played Steve Donahue. His character starts as part of the Donahue song and dance act, but he leaves to become ordained as a priest.

There's no business like show business...

Above: A production still from *There's No Business Like Show Business*. Marilyn's character of Vicky was given some of the production numbers written for Ethel Merman—which led to an interesting mixture of styles. Unlike the other lead actors, Marilyn was not a professional singer or dancer, but she worked hard with her coaches so her performance would measure up. Marilyn's routines were choreographed by Jack Cole with whom she had worked on *Gentlemen Prefer Blondes* but the others were created by Robert Alton.

Opposite: Marilyn with her drama coach, Natasha Lytess, during filming. Marilyn was only to do one further movie with her—*The Seven Year Itch* later in 1954. Natasha had tried to pressure Marilyn into doing *The Girl in Pink Tights*, and Joe DiMaggio

"After You Get What You Want...."

Opposite: The dress Marilyn wore for her performance of Irving Berlin's "After You Get What You Want You Don't Want It" in *There's No Business Like Show Business*, consisted of sequined white net over a flesh-colored body stocking, with strategically placed silver and white flowers and a slit high up onto the hip, masked with white fringing. Marilyn had recently signed an exclusive recording contract with RCA, so the movie soundtrack featured Broadway star Dolores Gray.

Above: Marilyn takes some time out to visit Merle Oberon on the set of her new picture, in which she was playing Napoleon's Josephine, and director Henry Koster entertains them both with a joke.

Left: Lewis K. Gough, past National Commander of the American Legion, presents Marilyn with a trophy and plaque in July 1954, for her morale-building activities on behalf of the armed forces.

Miss Modesty

Opposite: Backstage at the Martin Beck Theater, Marilyn has her eyes made up Oriental-style by actor David Wayne, as Joe looks on, amused. The two of them had been to see *The Teahouse of the August Moon*, in which Wayne starred.

Right: Ever willing to please, Marilyn adopts a pose for the photographers.

Following pages: Marilyn and Joe having dinner at El Morocco on East 54th Street in New York where Marilyn was on location filming *The Seven Year Itch*. Despite the smiles, Joe was deeply unhappy about his wife's continuing film career. He wanted her to settle down and be a wife—and hopefully a mother.

Joe objected strongly to Marilyn's habit of wearing revealing and low-cut dresses and in deference to him she often wore much more modest outfits during their brief marriage. He also disliked her going without underwear—and once made her wait in the powder room of a restaurant until suitable undergarments could be delivered. Despite these problems Marilyn found him deeply attractive—soon after they met she said of him, "He has the grace and beauty of a Michelangelo. He moves like a living statue."

The Seven Year Itch

The story is slight: husband Richard Sherman (Tom Ewell) is alone in New York during a sweltering summer, as his wife and young son have left for Maine. Sherman is determined to work, but is distracted by the arrival of "The Girl" (Marilyn), who has sublet one of his neighbor's apartments. Because of the heat, she walks around her apartment scantily dressed and keeps her "undies" in the icebox. He fantasizes about starting a relationship with her but she is more interested in his air-conditioned apartment—and is relieved to find that he is a married man so she feels safe with him!

Left: At the end of the movie, Sherman decides on fidelity and goes off, taking his son's canoe paddle, to join his wife and son, leaving Marilyn with the use of both the apartments.

Below: During one of the movie's fantasy sequences "The Girl" gets her toe caught in the tap and has to be freed by a plumber, played by Victor Moore.

Opposite: The heat wave that is an integral part of the plot was also an excuse for Marilyn to wear all kinds of skimpy costumes.

Working with Billy Wilder

Opposite: Marilyn discusses a scene with Billy Wilder on the set of *The Seven Year Itch*. Marilyn had been very keen to work with him—although that didn't stop her arriving late and requiring numerous retakes even when Wilder was happy. Wilder said of her later, "She is a very great actress. Better Marilyn late than most of the others on time." Marilyn often had difficulty remembering her lines so Wilder broke down scenes into smaller sequences to aid her. Despite this, the movie was almost two weeks behind schedule on November 4 when principal photography was finished.

Above: Marilyn with Tom Ewell, in a publicity still for the movie. Although Marilyn had been Wilder's first choice to play "The Girl" the role of Sherman had been more difficult to cast. Wilder had been favorably impressed by Walter Matthau's audition and Gary Cooper had also been seriously considered before the part was given to Tom Ewell who had begun his career in theater and had played Sherman in the original Broadway play.

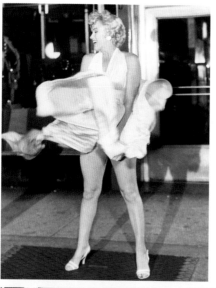

The famous skirt sequence

The shooting of the skirt-lifting scene on the street was as much about publicizing the movie as about getting the scene. The studio publicity department had leaked plans to the press, so by the time filming started there were hundreds of photographers and thousands of cheering onlookers. At least fifteen takes were done, leading Marilyn to comment to director Billy Wilder that she hoped they weren't for his private collection, to be screened at stag shows. The skirt blew up past Marilyn's waist several times—and even though she wore two pairs of panties the final shots were far too revealing to be used in the movie.

Unfortunately, Joe had been persuaded to come and watch the filming by his friend Walter Winchell. The sight of his wife displaying her underwear as thousands of men cheered was too much for him, and he left the scene looking visibly displeased. Back at the hotel that night he and Marilyn argued badly, and the next day he left New York for California.

Much of the footage taken on location on Lexington Avenue and 52nd Street was not used in the movie because of the background noise and poor light. The scene was shot again on a soundstage back at the Fox studio in Hollywood. The famous pleated, white halter-neck dress that Marilyn wore was part of a set of costumes designed by William Travilla, who had worked on Marilyn's costumes for *Gentlemen Prefer Blondes*.

A sense of sexuality

Above: Despite Sherman's fantasies, "The Girl" is entirely innocent and has no idea how he feels about her. Marilyn was superb at putting across a sense of sexuality with no apparent awareness of the effect she was having. Co-star Tom Ewell found her to be charming and courteous in real life—she even apologized for the taste of cough medicine on her breath during their kissing scene. She was taking it for a lung infection caught during the skirt-lifting sequence.

Opposite: Marilyn on the set of *The Seven Year Itch* in New York, with director Billy Wilder (left)

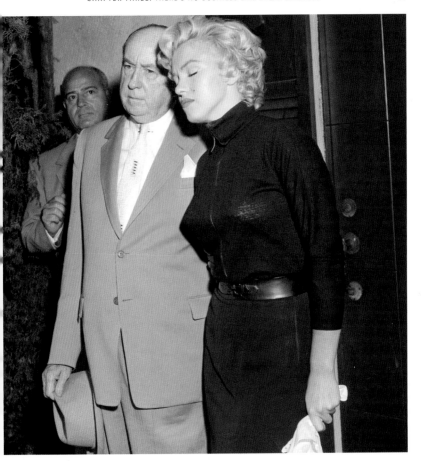

Spot the difference

Opposite: Europe's glamorous screen star Gina Lollobrigida had once said with some emphasis that she and Marilyn were quite different. This prompted Broadway columnist Earl Wilson to bring the two of them together at the Trans-Lux Theater in New York. Despite her view, the resulting picture reveals several similarities...

Above: Back in Hollywood, Marilyn was pictured with her attorney, Jerry Giesler, outside her Beverly Hills home. Newsmen were gathered to hear a statement, as studio publicist Harry Brand had recently announced that Marilyn was filing for divorce from the Yankee Clipper.

Heading for divorce...

Marilyn clings to Jerry Giesler for support as he gives an official statement to the press on October 6, 1954, revealing that she had filed a suit for divorce on the grounds of "mental cruelty" against Joe DiMaggio. As Marilyn posed for photographers she was obviously close to tears, and she refused to say a word herself, leaving all the talking to Giesler.

Everyone speculated about what had gone wrong after only nine months of marriage, as to outsiders they had seemed to be such a golden couple. Marilyn later described their marriage as a "sort of crazy, difficult friendship with sexual privileges. Later I learned that's what marriages often are."

Divorce granted

Opposite: In court in Santa Monica in California, before Judge Orlando H. Rhodes, Marilyn sat subdued and dressed all in black. She gave ten minutes of tearful testimony, alleging that Joe was "cold and indifferent, would get into moods and wouldn't speak to me for days at a time... if I tried to coax him to talk to me, he wouldn't answer me at all or he would say 'Leave me alone! Stop nagging me!'"

Left: Marilyn puts her signature to her divorce papers. There were tears in her eyes when the judge said, "Divorce granted." However, it was not final until the following year, October 1955. Joe refused to discuss the divorce action with the press, but privately he was reluctant to accept the proceedings as final, making several attempts to persuade Marilyn to change her mind.

Marilyn in hospital

Opposite: Marilyn poses for stills at the studio, although she was just about to go into the Cedars of Lebanon Hospital in Los Angeles for surgery to correct her chronic endometriosis.

Right: Although she tried to leave the hospital by the back door on November 12, 1954, newsmen were lying in wait to catch her looking tired and ill and far from her usual glamorous self. Despite the divorce, Joe practically lived at the hospital during the five days she was there, and visited her constantly at home in the early part of November. This started rumors that a reconciliation was on the cards—but Marilyn denied it.

Above: Newsmen and curious onlookers throng round as Marilyn leaves the Santa Monica Superior Court on October 27, 1954, followed by her attorney, Jerry Giesler.

Leaving LA

Left: Marilyn with Charlie Farrell at the Racquet Club in Palm Springs in December 1954. She was soon to leave for New York, where she was to remain for the whole of the following year—except for a brief trip back in early January 1955 to film additional dialogue for *The Seven Year Itch*. After consultations with a lawyer over her contract with Fox, Marilyn sacked her agent Charlie Feldman and announced that she and Greene had established their own company, Marilyn Monroe Productions.

Below: With Jacques Cemas, Sammy Davis Jr, Milton Greene, and Mel Tormé at The Mocambo in 1955, where they were celebrating Davis's return to show business after his accident.

Opposite: Marilyn dressed to face the New York winter weather.

New look Marilyn?

At a press conference to launch Marilyn Monroe Productions in January 1955 in New York, reporters were told to expect a "new and different" Marilyn, so they were rather disappointed when she appeared looking very much like the old model. She had bleached her hair a more platinum blonde and was dressed all in white, with a pure white mink, in an effort to look like Jean Harlow, as the first movie the new company intended to produce was Harlow's life story, with Marilyn in the lead role. The effect was rather lost on the assembled members of the press, who seemed more interested in whether the mink actually belonged to Marilyn;—she replied, "It's mine for the night."

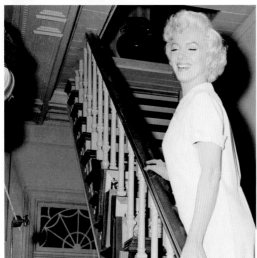

The press are not impressed

Opposite: Milton Greene and Marilyn had become sidetracked by the idea of portraying her as the ideal person to play Harlow, and the result was disastrous. The newspaper coverage the following day didn't even mention the formation of Marilyn Monroe Productions, instead being full of jokey comments, such as, "The new her didn't show up."

Left and above: Despite her estrangement from Twentieth Century Fox, Marilyn returned to Hollywood to reshoot one scene for *The Seven Year Itch*. Pausing on the staircase of the set, dressed in a nightgown and high-heeled slippers, she only had one line to say: "We can do this all summer." Afterwards she told newsmen that she hoped she could work out her differences with the studio and quipped that she was a changed woman—and might even start wearing underwear.

No reconciliation

Above: Marilyn with Joe DiMaggio, Joe's brother Dominic, and Dominic's wife, leaving a restaurant in Boston. Newsmen wanted to know if the meeting was a reconciliation, but Marilyn assured them it was not.

Left: While she was living in New York, Marilyn was involved in several campaigns to raise money for charity. Here she gives the press advance warning of the date of her appearance on the opening night of the circus, in aid of the New York Arthritis and Rheumatism Foundation.

Opposite: Publicity shot for *The Seven Year Itch*, which was soon to be released. At a party shortly after shooting finished, director Billy Wilder told Marilyn to stay with the character she had created, and to stop trying to move into more serious acting roles. Although she respected Wilder as a director, Marilyn had no intention of taking his advice.

A new career?

Marilyn hands a program to a rather surprised-looking Milton Berle (above), at the New York première of *East of Eden*, which starred James Dean. She was acting as a celebrity usherette in the Astor Theater, and the proceeds from the occasion were donated to the Actors Studio by director Elia Kazan.

Marilyn had recently become involved with the Actors Studio, both attending sessions there and privately studying drama with Lee Strasberg at his home. Although Strasberg was not impressed with the world of movies, feeling that stage acting was the only true medium, he was quick to use Marilyn's celebrity to earn additional money for the Studio and for himself personally. In Strasberg, Marilyn felt she had found someone who understood her needs and could offer her the opportunity to become a serious actress. She had conquered Hollywood but still craved the respect that she had imagined would come with stardom.

Taking the floor

Left: Marilyn takes the floor with Truman Capote at El Morocco in 1955—but seems rather distracted by something across the room. She and Capote had first met in 1950 and they became friends. He wanted Marilyn to play Holly Golightly in *Breakfast at Tiffany's*, but the part finally went to Audrey Hepburn—who was nominated for an Oscar as Best Actress in the role.

Attracting attention

Left: At the opening night of Tennessee Williams' play *Cat on a Hot Tin Roof*, Marilyn caught everyone's attention in a skin-tight sheath dress and a white mink. In New York Marilyn had an opportunity to change her life. She had been taken up by the literary set and was in great social demand. It was only a matter of time before she was to renew her acquaintance with Arthur Miller.

Above: Milton Berle, acting as the ringmaster of the Barnum & Bailey circus, gets an armful of Monroe charms at a rehearsal for her forthcoming appearance in aid of charity.

Just good friends

Above: The June 1955 première of *The Seven Year Itch* was a gala affair, with stars such as Grace Kelly, Henry Fonda, Eddie Fisher, and Richard Rodgers attending. To mark the occasion, a huge poster of Marilyn, in the famous skirt-lifting pose, was erected above Loew's State Theater in Times Square in New York. The original poster was replaced as there were complaints that it was too revealing. The image turned Marilyn into a vivid cultural icon, which still endures today. Marilyn was accompanied to the première by Joe, sparking rumors of a reconciliation, but she told reporters they were "just good friends." The movie went on to become the biggest hit of that summer, making a fortune for Fox—but Marilyn was still not paid her bonus as agreed.

The Prince and the Showgirl

At the beginning of 1956, Twentieth Century Fox issued a press release saying that they and Marilyn had finally come to terms, and that she would soon return to Hollywood. Many people had not really expected her to win and the victory made certain areas of the press begin to sit up and take notice of the "new" Marilyn—*Time* magazine even called her a "shrewd businesswoman." As if she felt that now she had reached a turning point, soon she legally changed her name to Marilyn Monroe.

Meanwhile, she stayed in New York, continuing her acting classes with Strasberg. Although she had been both studying and attending sessions she was not a member of the Actors Studio, which involved a formal audition and official approval. However, in February, Marilyn acted at the Studio in front of a proper audience for the first time, after Strasberg convinced her that she was ready. The scene chosen was the introductory one from *Anna Christie*, where Anna appears in a bar on her return home. It had already been made famous by Greta Garbo, since it was the opening scene in the Swedish star's first talking picture, and so became forever linked with the "Garbo talks!" advertisements. Before she went on, Marilyn was almost paralyzed with nerves, but once she began she performed perfectly, without forgetting any of her lines. Most people in the audience were astonished at the depth of her interpretation, and at the end they applauded. Marilyn was euphoric, but as usual—however well she had done—her delight never lasted, and self-doubt would soon gradually and insidiously return.

An important part of the new contract with Fox was that Marilyn would be able to make one independent movie a year. She fully intended to take advantage of this concession, and she had already begun talks with playwright Terence Rattigan and Laurence Olivier, with a view to appearing in a movie of *The Sleeping Prince*, which Olivier had performed on stage in London with his wife, Vivien Leigh, in 1953. Marilyn wanted to act with Olivier because she felt his reputation as one of the greatest English classical actors would finally make people regard her seriously as a performer. Olivier was keen to do the project because it would give him the opportunity to both co-produce and direct, and he hoped an association with Marilyn would revitalize his career. At a press conference in New York they announced their plans—but Marilyn upstaged everyone when the narrow strap on her dress broke, threatening to reveal more than was decent.

At the end of February, Marilyn returned to Hollywood. There they were to find her very much changed—she had taken on the system and won, she had learned self-possession and she certainly appeared much more self-confident. If she thought the events of the last year would bring her respect in the movie world, however, she soon found she was mistaken. Many saw her actions as evidence that she had tried to turn her back on Hollywood, which had put her where she was, while her interest in serious acting was regarded by her detractors as pretension, and not as a performer beginning to grow.

Opposite: Marilyn stands between Miller and Olivier.

As soon as she arrived back, Natasha Lytess tried to get in contact. However, Strasberg had sent his wife, Paula, to work with Marilyn instead, so Fox abruptly terminated Natasha's employment. Distraught and angry, she immediately tried to contact her former pupil, but she found that her notes were not answered and phone calls were not taken. Finally, in desperation, Natasha turned up at Marilyn's home. She was turned away at the door, but thought she saw Marilyn at the window. Soon afterward, she poured out her heart to the press, claiming that she had "created" Marilyn, and that she deserved better treatment. Natasha's presence had often caused dissension on set, and on later movies others suspected that—rather than helping—she had fed Marilyn's insecurity by demanding retakes when they were not necessary. Marilyn may have needed Natasha, but the reverse was also true. When it came down to it, Marilyn becoming self-confident enough to be able to function without her was not really in Natasha's interest. Unfortunately for her, Marilyn believed that she had been let down, and she had no hesitation in dropping her former coach, now that she had an acceptable alternative.

Marilyn had returned to start work on *Bus Stop*, the movie of a Broadway hit. This was the first picture that Marilyn was to undertake at Fox after achieving her newly won power, and studio bosses were worried about what impossible demands she might make. When she first saw the elaborate costumes that had been designed for her role, she dismissed them as totally unsuitable, and everyone immediately feared the worst. To their surprise, Marilyn suggested that they should look round the costume department, and she picked out a series of shabby, second-hand outfits that she felt were more appropriate for a down-at-heel bar room girl. Director Joshua Logan was delighted—he had been reluctant to take the project initially, as he had believed that Marilyn couldn't act. He was convinced otherwise by speaking to Strasberg, who had given her a glowing testimony, and now here was evidence that Marilyn really was taking her role seriously. Alone of all her directors, he planned alternative shooting schedules to allow for the occasions when Marilyn was late, which cut down tension on the set considerably.

However, this amicable relationship with her director was not mirrored with Marilyn's co-stars, Don Murray and Hope Lange. Marilyn was annoyed that Murray was impervious to her charms, seeming more interested in Lange—whom he later married. As for Lange, Marilyn insisted that her blonde hair be dyed darker, so as not to compete with her own bright tresses; one of the downsides of Marilyn's new-found power was that her ever-present insecurity could be allowed free rein.

Despite this, Marilyn worked hard, first on location in the desert near Phoenix, Arizona, and then in the mountains at Sun Valley, Idaho. The difference in temperature, coupled with the light clothes she wore in character, brought her down with such a severe case of bronchitis that she had to be hospitalized. She was kept in hospital for four days before she was allowed back to work.

On her return, she faced one of the most important scenes of the movie—Cherie's monologue about her life. Marilyn was renowned for being unable to remember lines, and this was a long speech. Logan knew she would not be able to do it in one take, which raised a second problem: the time she needed to psych herself up to perform. He resolved both problems by keeping the camera running take after take, without ever calling "Cut!". As he had hoped, Marilyn just kept going, and he was able to piece together all the best bits to create a stunning and moving scene. Marilyn was delighted because she had proved she was able to handle complicated dialogue.

While filming was in progress, Arthur Miller had been staying in Reno, Nevada, establishing residency so he could obtain a divorce. While they were apart Marilyn kept in touch with long phone calls, but the day after his divorce was finalized they met up in New York. Miller had another problem. He had applied for a passport to go to England partly to accompany Marilyn when she went to film *The Sleeping Prince*, and also because his play, *A View from the Bridge*, was about to be staged there. However, he had been briefly associated with the Communist Party many years before, and had already been turned down for a passport on a previous occasion—and it was now the height of the McCarthy witch-hunts against Communism. He was called to appear before the House UnAmerican Activities Committee to testify, and he co-operated fully—except that he refused to name names. Despite this, he was at first not held in contempt, as many others taking a similar stance had been—to some extent because everyone was distracted by his announcement that he intended to marry Marilyn.

As the news of the impending nuptials spread, newsmen and photographers camped outside their door, and followed them everywhere they went, even after they left New York for the Miller family home at Roxbury, Connecticut. Marilyn was used to such attention, but Miller was not. He was also not the kind of writer who could work in any surroundings, and in these conditions he found it impossible to produce the rewrites he was under a deadline to complete. Finally they married in secret, in a judge's chambers just over the state line in White Plains, New York, followed by a Jewish ceremony, also in secret, in New York. After the event Miller hoped that everyone could go back to normal life. Little did he know that his life with Marilyn would never be normal.

Two weeks later, after Miller finally obtained his passport, he and Marilyn arrived in England. *The Sleeping Prince* was to be filmed as *The Prince and the Showgirl*, but the project was not a good experience for most of those concerned. The first problem had come up before they even left America—Strasberg demanded that his wife, Paula, be paid a guaranteed salary of $25,000 for ten weeks' work plus expenses—far more than anyone else on the movie except Olivier and Marilyn herself. When Milton Greene, Marilyn's business partner, understandably objected to this, Strasberg simply pointed out how fragile Marilyn was, and said that he would accept a percentage of the movie's profits instead. Apart from using her to improve his financial situation, many believe that Strasberg also manipulated her for his own ends. Marilyn was his most high-profile pupil, and he was seemingly determined that he alone would get the credit for her achievements. Far from really supporting her on *The Prince and the Showgirl*, he constantly criticized Olivier—who regarded Method acting with contempt—in long telephone calls from New York, while Olivier's direction of Marilyn was undermined by Paula Strasberg on set.

As for Olivier himself, apart from his problems with Paula Strasberg he was exasperated by Marilyn's lateness and difficulty in remembering lines, and was frustrated by his inability to get through to her. Marilyn had been excited about working with such a famous and respected actor, but now she was afraid he would ruin her performance. She thought he was condescending much of the time—particularly after he told her before one scene to "be sexy." For her, the movie had never been about "being sexy"—it was about being accepted as a serious performer. In this she had misjudged the material, because in fact the role called for exactly the kind of beautiful, uncomplicated, and seductive blonde that she had played so well so many times in the past.

On top of all this, Marilyn and Miller's marriage was already in some trouble—it was the first time the two of them had spent extended time together, and the first time Miller had had to deal at first hand with her work anxieties, sleeplessness, and insecurity. Marilyn the person had turned out to be quite different from Marilyn the fantasy. Miller was in the habit of jotting down stray thoughts for use in later work, and apparently Marilyn read some of them, which had led her to doubt that Miller really did love her. From that moment on, she never felt quite so safe and secure in Miller's love as she had done before. There was further unhappiness in their marriage when toward the end of August, Marilyn became pregnant with a much-wanted child, but miscarried the baby within a few weeks.

Marilyn had also come to distrust her business partner, Milton Greene. Greene and Miller had always disliked and distrusted one another, each resenting the influence the other had on Marilyn. Greene was not happy that Miller intended to be actively involved in Marilyn Monroe Productions. In turn, Miller had no faith in Greene's abilities, and he tried to convince Marilyn that she didn't need him. As for Marilyn herself, she came to suspect that Greene was working against her, not supporting her in arguments with others on set and going along with cuts of her scenes. All in all, it was a miracle that *The Prince and the Showgirl* came in under budget and more or less on time.

The Prince and the Showgirl

Opposite: At a press conference at the Plaza Hotel in New York in February 1956, Marilyn and Laurence Olivier announced their intention to make a movie version of Terence Rattigan's *The Sleeping Prince*. They planned to film in England, where Olivier had had a hit on the London stage with the original play, in which he had starred with his wife, Vivien Leigh. Marilyn had agreed to pay $125,000 for the movie rights and an additional sum for Rattigan to write the screenplay.

Above: Marilyn chats to James Cagney. The Hollywood press was full of stories about her return to the fold and news of her latest project.

Stealing the show

Above: Marilyn leans forward to speak to eager reporters, telling them, "I'd like to continue my growth in every way possible."

Opposite: Although she looked quite demure in her outfit, complete with coat, scarf, and gloves, during the course of the interview the spaghetti strap of Marilyn's dress broke, instantly drawing everyone's attention. Olivier was convinced it had been done on purpose, but it certainly guaranteed that they were both front-page news the following day.

Mesmerized

Above: Marilyn and Susan Strasberg, daughter of Marilyn's mentor
Lee Strasberg, seem mesmerized by Laurence Olivier. The three were
backstage at the Cort Theater in New York, where Susan was appearing
in *The Diary of Anne Frank*.

Returning in triumph

Above: At the end of February 1956, Marilyn poses for photographers as she boards a plane in New York to return to Hollywood. She had been away from the movie capital of America for over a year, as negotiations were carried out to resolve her contract dispute with Fox. Most people had felt she would not win her battle with the studio, but now she was returning in triumph having obtained several concessions that were unique at the time—including a percentage of the profits, and approval of script, director, and cinematographer.

Left: Marilyn looks pleased with the way her life is going.

Seriously smart

Left: Despite what reporters might have said, there was no denying that Marilyn looked both seriously smart and glamorous in her new wardrobe of tailored suits and matching gloves.

Above: Both Marilyn and Jack Warner look delighted as it is announced that she is to co-star with Laurence Olivier in the movie of *The Sleeping Prince* for Warner Brothers.

Fined!

Left: Marilyn appears in court in Beverly Hills, charged with driving without a license. The offense had taken place back in 1954 when she was first becoming famous, but the judge was not impressed and lectured her severely before imposing a $56 fine.

Opposite: In court, awaiting her turn before the bench, with attorney, Irving L. Stein.

Below: Milton Greene, vice-president of Marilyn's independent production company, faces the press with her just after she returned to Hollywood following her long exile in New York. Marilyn Monroe Productions and Fox had recently come to terms, so Marilyn had returned in triumph.

Bus Stop

Marilyn as Cherie. The first movie she was scheduled to make for Fox was *Bus Stop,* which was based on a Broadway hit written by William Inge. When the play was adapted for the screen, writer George Axelrod bore Marilyn in mind and added details from her own life. Joshua Logan, who was on the list of 16 directors approved by Marilyn, was well versed in Stanislavsky and The Method and had a reputation as a talented director of sensitive actors.

Although Logan was patient and tried to accommodate Marilyn's needs, he had a tough time keeping the production on schedule. As before, she found it difficult to remember her lines and spent hours in her dressing room before being able to face the camera. Paula Strasberg had replaced Natasha Lytess as Marilyn's acting coach but although Logan liked her on a personal level, he was not about to have his authority on set undermined and at first confined her to Marilyn's dressing room.

Posing on set

Left: Marilyn plays Cherie, a down-at-heel bar room singer, with Don Murray as Bo Decker, her devoted admirer. On set Don Murray did not always find it easy to work with Marilyn. While shooting the scene where Cherie tries to leave Bo, one of Marilyn's improvised gestures cut Murray's eyelid but Marilyn failed to apologize.

Marilyn vetoed the elaborate costumes originally designed for the part, and picked out some tattered clothes from the studio wardrobe instead, which she felt would be more in keeping with her character. Much of the look of the movie was designed by Milton Greene, who had a wonderful eye for what would work on camera.

Opposite: Marilyn with Arthur O'Connell, who played Virgil Blassing, the young cowboy's older and wiser guardian.

Mr President

Opposite: At a party thrown by Joshua Logan, director of *Bus Stop*, Marilyn was introduced to Indonesian President Sukarno. He had particularly asked to meet her because he was interested in Hollywood and her movies were very popular in his country. The party also marked Marilyn's 30th birthday.

Above: At a press conference, the journalists may all have their heads down but Marilyn—as usual—knows exactly where the camera is.

Right: A kiss for the photographer. Marilyn was far better with stills photographers than she was on a movie set—she didn't feel the same pressure to perform, but was still able to conjure up her star persona for the camera. By the time work on *Bus Stop* had finished at the end of May 1956 she was physically and emotionally exhausted. Marilyn had felt the need to show her year with Strasberg had made a difference to her performance and, in addition to this, filming in the desert of Arizona and the cold in Sun Valley had put a strain on her health.

Happy birthday

Arriving on June 2 at Idlewild Airport in New York on a flight from the west coast, Marilyn is presented with a birthday cake in her limousine. She had celebrated her 30th birthday the previous day in Hollywood. Reporters wanted to know about her romance with playwright Arthur Miller, but she just smiled mysteriously and blew them a kiss.

Mrs Arthur Miller

While Marilyn had been filming *Bus Stop*, Miller had spent some six weeks in Nevada in order to obtain his divorce. He had been called to appear before the House UnAmerican Activities Committee to answer questions about his past association with the Communist Party and had revealed to the Committee that he wanted a passport so he could go to England to "be there with the woman who will then be my wife." Washington reporters descended upon him and he told them that he expected to marry Marilyn within "a day or two," adding that whether or not he got his passport, Marilyn would be going to London as Mrs Arthur Miller.

Reporters then rushed to the apartment on Sutton Place, where Marilyn had been keeping out of sight, to ask for her side of the story. Until then she had refused to be interviewed, afraid of saying the wrong thing and damaging Miller's chances, but now she called an impromptu press conference and told reporters how happy she was to be getting married.

Two lovebirds

On June 22, 1956 Marilyn and Arthur Miller appeared before the press together in front of the Sutton Place apartment, where they were staying in New York, to talk about their forthcoming wedding. They told reporters they planned a simple ceremony; they had not yet set the date, but it would be "sometime in July." At one point Marilyn hugged Miller so hard that he had to tell her to stop, "or I'll fall over." Following comments by Francis Walter, chairman of the HUAC, reporters asked Miller if he would enjoy his honeymoon in America if he did not get his passport, but Miller pointed out that it would be difficult to do so, as Marilyn was already committed to going to England.

In the country

It soon became apparent that reporters would give them no peace, so the happy couple left for Miller's home in Roxbury, Connecticut. Unfortunately the press soon followed them there. To try to keep them at bay, a photocall was arranged and Miller and Marilyn appeared, casually dressed. They told reporters that there would be no wedding for several days, and Miller appealed to them to go away for a short while and allow Marilyn to get some rest. He promised an announcement the following Friday.

A bad omen

Opposite above: Marilyn rushes past reporters, ashen-faced and shaking, after witnessing a terrible car accident nearby. Journalist Mara Scherbatoff had been following them in a car driven by the young brother of her photographer, who had lost control and crashed into a tree. The boy had some injuries, but Scherbatoff was seriously hurt and she later died in hospital. Miller had had enough of the media circus, and he brought the wedding forward to that evening, arranging for the ceremony to be held at the Westchester County Court House in White Plains, New York, with Judge Seymour Robinowitz officiating.

Above and opposite below: The day after the civil ceremony, the newlyweds looked happy and carefree as they left for a romantic picnic together—although Marilyn privately believed that the death on the very day of her wedding was a bad omen.

Next door to the Queen

A limousine took the Millers to Surrey, along with Milton Greene, while the Oliviers followed in a second car. A grand Georgian mansion, Parkside House, had been rented for Marilyn and Arthur Miller to stay in. It was situated right next to Windsor Great Park—with a private gate into the park itself. A long drive ensured some privacy, but Marilyn insisted that a group of photographers were allowed up to the house immediately, and that they should all pose for a few more pictures—even though a proper press conference had been scheduled for the following day. Although Vivien Leigh smiled bravely, she was clearly somewhat unhappy at being asked to pose next to a woman twelve years her junior, who was renowned for her attractiveness to men, particularly as the Oliviers' marriage had been going through a rocky patch of late.

Another day, another press conference

Opposite: Marilyn was delighted that Miller was apparently willing to support her publicly as she geared herself up to begin work. Unfortunately he had never seen this side of her, and it wasn't long before he began to wonder just what he had taken on.

Above and left: Despite a promise to Olivier, Marilyn arrived over an hour late for a press conference that had been arranged in the Lancaster Room of the Savoy Hotel in London. Olivier had entertained journalists alone while they all waited, and he was not in the best of moods. However, as usual, Marilyn charmed everyone into forgiving her. Previously Olivier had said that he had planned to fall "most shatteringly in love" with Marilyn, but now she was married to Arthur Miller, and he and Vivien were expecting a child together—which might signal a new start in their troubled marriage. He therefore was far more reserved with Marilyn than he had been in New York, which she found very unsettling.

In London

Below and right: Interest in Marilyn was at fever pitch in London, and crowds turned out to see her whenever she appeared in public. Despite the fact that this was often very intrusive, she was always aware that she owed her fans a great deal. If she chose not to turn on her Marilyn persona, she could often pass unnoticed in a crowd. Despite this, when she and Arthur Miller went to the theater—which they did quite often in London—the number of people who turned out to see them was so great that the police had to be called to clear a path for them to enter and leave the building. Marilyn was used to this kind of public furor, but Miller found it very hard to adapt to it.

Opposite: Olivier and Marilyn share a quiet word at yet another press conference. They apparently got on famously at these affairs, complimenting each other and appearing to enjoy working together, but unfortunately this happy atmosphere was not destined to last long once filming began.

The happy couple

Although they were seemingly enjoying a carefree time in London, both Marilyn and her husband were aware that Congress was about to vote on whether to cite Miller for contempt. Although he had his passport, his problems with the HUAC had not gone away by any means.

Tension on set

Above: Marilyn with Olivier on set. Problems on the set of *The Prince and the Showgirl* began almost at once. Olivier did not believe in Method acting, and Marilyn came to mistrust him, particularly after he instructed her to "be sexy" for one scene. Although he was not present in person, Marilyn's mentor, Lee Strasberg, had sent his wife Paula as Marilyn's drama coach and she took every opportunity to undermine Olivier's direction. Marilyn was unwell during most of filming: fearful of failure in front of the camera, she was using alcohol and prescription drugs to help her cope with her anxieties. However, even when she arrived on set looking disheveled after a sleepless night, the combination of Marilyn's ability to sparkle for the camera and the skill of cinematographer Jack Cardiff, who had worked on *The Red Shoes* and *Black Narcissus*, managed to produce a stunning image.

Opposite: Vivien Leigh was appearing in *South Sea Bubble*, and Marilyn and Miller went to the Lyric Theatre to see a performance. After the show they walked hand-in-hand through an excited crowd.

Right: Marilyn photographed at the theater.

Royal command

Above: Marilyn arrives at a dressmaker to collect her outfit in which to be presented to Queen Elizabeth II at the Royal Command Performance of *The Battle of the River Plate* in London, in October 1956. She went in looking pale and timid, but emerged poised, confident, and glittering in a gold dress.

Left: Towards the end of August 1956, Miller decided to fly back to America for a few days to see his children. The trip was intended to be a secret—the name on his ticket was Mr Stevenson—as there was always a possibility that his return to America would precipitate more problems with the HUAC.

Opposite: The Millers leave the Palace Theatre by the stage door, after seeing Brecht's *Caucasian Chalk Circle* performed in German. This was Marilyn's first night out after recovering from a miscarriage, but it was also the couple's celebration of Miller's return from America. They arrived late and a surprised management ushered them into seats in the stalls.

At the Comedy

Left and below: The opening night of *A View from the Bridge* was held at the Comedy Theatre, but it was performed before the members of a newly created private theater club—the New Watergate Theatre Club. The Lord Chamberlain had objected to a scene in which one man kissed another on the lips, and had refused to grant the necessary permit for public performance. Both Marilyn and her husband had to become members of the club before they were allowed inside to see the play—even though he was the author. Marilyn had recently been ill, but she was still determined to appear. Both the Millers obviously enjoyed the performance. The story was of particular personal significance to Miller at the time, as it involves a man's decision to betray his friends, which leads to his destruction.

Opposite: Marilyn signs her application form for membership.

Opening night

Vivien Leigh, Laurence Olivier, Marilyn, and Miller take their seats for the black tie première of *A View from the Bridge*. Marilyn wore a scarlet satin gown so tight around the knees that walking was an achievement. As a result of her attendance the publicity for the play was tremendous, and promoter Binkie Beaumont had signed up over 13,000 members to his hastily formed theater club–pocketing the small membership fee. Many members of the audience were more interested in studying Marilyn than watching the play, but it proved to be a success and was well reviewed.

Putting on a show

Backstage at the première of *A View from the Bridge*. Marilyn felt that she had lost some part of Miller's love, and she was now working hard to win it back. She had miscarried their baby and she had read somes notes he had jotted down which, she felt, showed he regretted having married her. He found her needs hard to cope with, and her constant demands were interfering with his work as a writer and so he had withdrawn somewhat. There were misunderstandings on both sides—he did not appreciate how much she dreaded being abandoned, and she did not understand that a writer may draw on real life, but is not necessarily expressing how he personally feels in his characters' views.

Kisses

On November 20, 1956 the Oliviers saw the Millers off at London Airport. It was kisses all round as everyone agreed that they had to put on a good face in public for the sake of the movie. It was not only the Millers who were going home disillusioned—Olivier was disappointed that he had apparently missed an opportunity to revive his flagging career, while Vivien had also lost her baby—and as it turned out, her last chance to save the marriage. She and Marilyn had totally failed to develop any kind of rapport, and during the time in England they had only met on formal occasions.

After his experience on this movie, Olivier considered Marilyn a "thoroughly ill-mannered and rude girl," but years later he said, "Maybe I was tetchy with Marilyn and with myself, because I felt my career was in a rut... I was as good as could be, and, Marilyn! Marilyn was quite wonderful, the best of all."

CHAPTER FIVE

Some Like It Hot

While Marilyn had been away in England, *Bus Stop* had been released. She had seen a rough cut of the movie in London, and had been devastated because part of her performance had been cut, and much of the dramatic monologue that she was so proud of had ended up on the cutting-room floor. She had wanted Miller and Strasberg to see her achievement, and now they never would. She also felt that the cuts had ruined her chances of an Oscar nomination— and what was all the more galling was that Don Murray was nominated as Best Supporting Actor, and as Most Promising Newcomer for the British Academy Awards. She turned on director Joshua Logan, berating him for spoiling her performance, but in fact he had fought to keep much of the material and been overruled by studio bosses, who felt the movie was too long. Despite this, the reviews were glowing, with almost every newspaper critic commenting that Marilyn had proved that she really could act.

Back in New York at the beginning of 1957, the rough cut of *The Prince and the Showgirl* did not initially look quite as good, and when it was first released later in the year the reviews were mixed. However, it picked up five nominations for the British Academy Awards, including Best Foreign Actress for Marilyn. In the event, she did not win, but in 1959 it did bring her Italy's most prestigious acting award—the David Di Donatello statuette for Best Actress in a Foreign Film. Many critics now regard it as one of her finest performances, and she easily steals the movie from Olivier. However, at the time Marilyn felt that Milton Greene had let her down with their first independent production,

and Miller fueled this view, finally convincing her that she no longer needed Greene. As a result, Greene was fired from Marilyn Monroe Productions and a new board of directors was appointed. He may have made mistakes, but it was a poor return for a man who had practically given up his own career to help Marilyn, who had supported her financially when she was on suspension throughout the greater part of 1955, and who had helped her achieve her revised contract with Fox. Much later, Marilyn confessed to Greene's wife, Amy, that Milton was the only man she had ever trusted, but that Miller had driven him away and she had felt unable to resist. The truth was that at the time, Marilyn was more concerned with making a success of her shaky marriage.

After all the draining experiences in England, she now wanted to take some time off. Her contract with Fox called for her to make four movies for them within seven years, of which she had so far completed one. There were plans for her to appear in a remake of *The Blue Angel* but despite prolonged negotiations on both sides the idea was eventually shelved. Until Fox came up with an acceptable project, she could choose whether to work or not. She decided that what she really wanted to do was to try to be a good wife: to create a proper home for Miller, where he could work in peace, and to have a baby. For the moment she put her own work on hold and concentrated on furnishing their new apartment in New York, while she also began treatment at Doctors Hospital to enable her to carry a baby to term.

Opposite: A publicity shot, taken by Frank Powolny.

Meanwhile, events from the past were coming back to haunt both Miller and Marilyn's ex-husband, Joe DiMaggio. First of all, in February 1957 Miller was finally indicted by a federal grand jury on two counts of contempt of Congress, as a result of his failure to name names at his House UnAmerican Activities Committee hearing in 1956. If he was proved guilty, each count could mean a huge fine and up to a year in prison. His lawyers were confident that he would win, because the questions he had refused to answer were actually nothing to do with what the HUAC was supposed to be investigating, namely the abuse of passports. Despite this, Miller was too stressed to concentrate on his work, partly because of the legal proceedings hanging over him, and also because his defense would run up huge legal fees.

As for DiMaggio, an event that had happened in 1954, just after his divorce from Marilyn had been granted, now suddenly and unexpectedly hit the news. After they separated, DiMaggio had hired a private detective to follow Marilyn, and had come to the conclusion that she was having an affair with her voice coach, Hal Schaefer. In early November, DiMaggio and Frank Sinatra were having a drink together when news came that Marilyn's car had been seen parked outside an apartment building. DiMaggio and Sinatra joined the detective and his associate outside, and the four of them broke into one of the apartments, expecting to catch Marilyn *in flagrante delecto*. However, they had the wrong apartment—they had broken down the door of Florence Kee. The noise had alerted the rest of the building, so Marilyn, who was apparently having dinner with Schaefer and another woman next door, escaped without being seen. At the time, Sinatra managed to keep his and DiMaggio's name out of the newspapers, but many months later the full story of the event which had become known as the "Wrong Door" raid was published in *Confidential* magazine. Kee promptly sued her famous intruders, but the case dragged on for years, so Sinatra was not called to testify until early 1957. The newspapers had a field day, but eventually DiMaggio settled out of court.

Unfortunately, Miller's legal problems were not to be settled so easily. Marilyn went with him to Washington,

although by now she was again pregnant. Reporters swarmed over the Federal District Court to see her, but she was keeping out of sight and Miller explained that he thought that everyone should stay focused on the issue at hand. After that, journalists tried to contact Marilyn at the house where the Millers were staying. Finally she appeared to speak to them, clearly stating her support for her husband. At the end of a six-day hearing, the defendant was found guilty on both counts, though soon afterwards the judge revised his verdict to a conviction on only one charge, for which Miller was fined $500 and received a suspended sentence of one month. His lawyers instantly appealed, and in a much more hopeful mood he and Marilyn left to spend the summer on Long Island.

Their happiness was short-lived—just over two months later Marilyn collapsed and was rushed by ambulance to Doctors Hospital in New York. Her much-wanted pregnancy had turned out to be ectopic, and had to be terminated to save her life. However, apart from the natural sadness of losing her baby, she also felt a failure as a wife because she was not able to give Miller a child, and she now seemed convinced that sooner or later he would leave her. Shortly afterwards, she took an overdose of sleeping pills, but Miller found her and called for help. In an attempt to convince her that he still loved her, he started work on turning his short story, *The Misfits*, into a screenplay for her. Unfortunately, Marilyn did not take this gesture in quite the way in which it was intended. Now that Miller was busy working he cut himself off at the very moment when she needed emotional support, and—what was even worse—she began to suspect that he was only staying with her to get his screenplay accepted and revive his flagging writing career.

At the beginning of 1958, Twentieth Century Fox began to panic that they had let a year go by without getting another Marilyn Monroe movie. They had no intention of accepting *The Misfits* as a potential project until Miller's conviction was overturned, and there was no sign in the immediate future of that happening. However, they had nothing else that Marilyn was prepared to consider. Meanwhile, director Billy Wilder sent her the script for *Some Like It Hot*. The story was set in 1929, and involves two musicians, who inadvertently witness the St Valentine's Day Massacre and have to hide from the Mob. They disguise themselves as women and join an all-girl band, led by singer and ukulele player Sugar Kane. Marilyn was initially not interested in the part, because in the movie Sugar never realizes that the two "girls" are men, which Marilyn felt was taking the concept of being a "dumb blonde" to a ridiculous extreme. And had she not fought to get away from being cast in dumb blonde roles? Miller, however, pointed out that the script was outstanding, and would be a sure-fire winner. Both her agents and Fox agreed. Even though the movie was to be made by the Mirisch brothers and distributed by United Artists so they wouldn't make a penny from it, Fox felt it was in their interest to get Marilyn back to work—and if the movie was a success, it would enhance her value as a Fox property.

Finally, Marilyn gave in and signed the contract. Again Paula Strasberg was hired as dramatic coach. Billy Wilder soon exerted his authority on set and put Paula firmly in her place, although he welcomed her support of Marilyn. He also admired Marilyn's sense of comedy, and was prepared to listen to her ideas with respect. It was apparently her idea to change Sugar's first appearance to establish her kooky nature from the outset, so the train suddenly lets off a puff of steam as she teeters down the platform on her high heels, making her jump and the audience laugh. Despite these good omens, Marilyn was soon arriving late, demanding retakes and forgetting her lines. As well as her old demons, she now had to cope with an increasing intake of prescribed drugs: sleeping pills to get her to sleep, uppers to wake her up, and tranquillizers to calm her down. Wilder said later that the experience of working on the project brought him to the verge of a breakdown—and although the end result turned out to be worth it, at the time he had not believed there would be a final product.

As an added complication, towards the end of shooting, Marilyn again became pregnant. Luckily the most strenuous parts of the movie had already been filmed, but Marilyn took every opportunity to rest in an attempt to carry the baby to term. However, in December she miscarried this baby too—it was her last attempt to become a mother.

In March 1959, *Some Like It Hot* had its première. It was an instant success, both with the critics and at the box office. It not only outgrossed all other movies in the first half of 1959, but also established a box office record for any comedy that remained unbroken for many years. It is fondly regarded as Marilyn's best movie by many of her fans, and is still shown regularly.

Despite this massive success, 1959 was to be another year when Marilyn made no movies. Fox was aware that, according to her contract, they had to put her in a movie by April 14, or lose the right to one of the four pictures they were entitled to. She was assigned to *Time and Tide*, a script based on novels by William Bradford, to be directed by Elia Kazan. She was due to start work on April 14, but when Kazan came on board he demanded extensive rewrites, so Marilyn was instructed to remain in New York until they needed her—although her salary would be paid from the original start date. Meanwhile, Kazan decided he didn't want to cast Marilyn, but preferred Lee Remick. Fox had failed to notice that Marilyn's contract specified that filming had to start ten weeks from her official start date—which was April 14—so they were surprised to receive notification from her lawyer on June 25 that she was no longer obliged to appear in *Time and Tide*. What was worse, she wanted payment for the picture, as per the terms of her contract, even though she hadn't worked on it, and was insisting she be released from one of the movies she owed. The studio's legal department confirmed that all these demands were in accordance with her contract: Fox should have asked for an extension, and had failed to do so. Marilyn was a really hot property after the success of *Some Like It Hot*, and they now had another project for her—and as a result, all her demands were met—yet again Marilyn had taken on the studio and won.

The new movie was *The Billionaire*, co-starring Gregory Peck and to be directed by George Cukor. Marilyn was scheduled to start work in October rehearsing her musical numbers. However, filming didn't start until early in 1960 and by then Gregory Peck had dropped out after the script was altered to build Marilyn's role, and her new co-star was French sex symbol Yves Montand.

A cheerful wave

Opposite: Marilyn waves to newsmen through the window of the car, as she is driven away. She always made a big effort to be co-operative with the press and had quickly developed the skill of turning the coverage to her best advantage. She cultivated allies in the press—notably Sidney Skolsky, who not only wrote favorably about her in his column, but also helped her to write articles that were published under her own name.

Above: At the première of *The Prince and the Showgirl* at New York's Radio City Music Hall, Marilyn stops to admire one of the elaborately uniformed soldiers on display. Reviews of the movie were mixed at the time, but Marilyn's performance later became regarded as one of her finest.

Family business

Above: When Arthur Miller was put on trial for contempt of Congress in Washington, Marilyn accompanied him but stayed out of sight until the trial was over. When she finally did agree to speak to reporters, she told them she had spent the time reading transcripts of the proceedings in court.

Left: Actress Joan Copeland was Arthur Miller's sister, and when she opened in Noel Coward's *Conversation Piece*, Marilyn went to the first night party in the Barbizon Plaza Hotel to congratulate her sister-in-law.

Opposite: Marilyn with society hostess Elsa Maxwell at an April in Paris Ball, held in 1957.

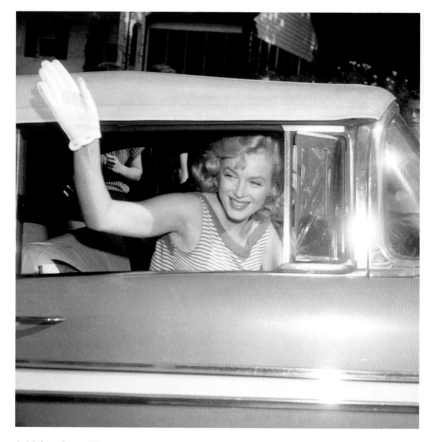

A visit from the stork?

Above: In April 1957, Marilyn had found out she was expecting a baby. Her doctor had warned her that it might be an ectopic pregnancy, in which the fetus develops inside a fallopian tube instead of in the uterus, but she had put such thoughts out of her head and was euphoric at the thought of finally becoming a mother.

Opposite above: Onlookers laugh as Marilyn lights a super firecracker to start inaugual ceremonies at the reactivated Rockefeller Center Sidewalk Superintendents Club in New York. The firecracker triggered a dynamite blast in the excavation pit of the new 47-story Time & Life building nearby.

Opposite below: Marilyn and her husband refuse to be drawn on whether she is pregnant, as they arrive back in New York after a short vacation in Jamaica.

Putting
on a brave face

Although she was
depressed when the
pregnancy did turn out
to be ectopic and had to
be terminated, Marilyn
still managed to put on
a brave and happy face
for newsmen as she left
Doctors Hospital in New
York with Arthur Miller in
August 1957.

Signing up

Left: Harold Mirisch, president of the Mirisch Company, talks to Marilyn about their upcoming production, *Some Like It Hot*, Billy Wilder and I.A.L. Diamond's screenplay based on a German movie entitled *Fanfares of Love*. Marilyn's role was supposed to be peripheral to the main action, but the minute she arrives on screen she seems to take over the movie. Despite her misgivings about playing another dumb blonde, she needed a hit when *The Prince and the Showgirl* did not do as well as expected.

Following pages: When Arthur Miller was inducted as a member of the National Institute of Arts and Letters on May 21, 1958, Marilyn happily signed autographs for her fans.

Helping others

Left and below: At the 1958 March of Dimes Fashion Show, Marilyn appeared as one of the models and was pictured with twins Lindy and Sandy Sue Solomon, who were featured on the March of Dimes poster. The charity helped children with polio, and one of the twins walked with crutches after recovering from the illness. The fashion show was held at the Waldorf-Astoria and it featured designs by members of the couture group of the New York Dress Institute, as well as other designers from New York, California, and Italy. Marilyn wore a champagne-colored silk dress with a fitted jacket designed by John Moore for Talmack.

Some Like It Hot

Opposite: Marilyn and Arthur Miller leaving New York for Hollywood, where Marilyn was to start work on *Some like It Hot*.

Above: Co-star Tony Curtis had to spend almost the entire movie in drag, since the plot involved two male musicians who witness the St Valentine's Day Massacre in 1920s New York and disguise themselves as women to escape the Mob. Curtis was uncomfortable in costume at first, but with the help of drag artist Barbette quickly learned how to walk like a woman. Lemmon was not so adept a pupil.

Right: Director Billy Wilder discusses a scene with Marilyn. She had been dismayed to discover the movie was being shot in black and white, rather than Technicolor, as per her contract with Fox. Wilder explained that tests had shown that the thick makeup Tony Curtis and Jack Lemmon had to wear in their guise as women turned greenish when filmed in color, making them look like clowns.

Casting Sugar

Above and opposite: Marilyn as
Sugar, the ukelele player in the "all-
girl" band. Wilder had considered
several actors for the male leads
in *Some Like It Hot*, including Frank
Sinatra and at an early stage Danny
Kaye and Bob Hope, before settling
on Curtis and then Lemmon.
Despite difficulties on *The Seven
Year Itch*, Wilder rated Marilyn's
performance highly and cast her in
the role of Sugar considering it the
weakest role and therefore vital to
chose the right actress for the part.
Filming began in early September
1958 but Wilder and Diamond
continued to work on the script
during shooting.

Right: Joe E. Brown, who played
millionaire Osgood Fielding III, chats
with Marilyn on set. Fielding falls in
love with "Daphne"—Jack Lemmon
in drag.

Working with Paula

Right: Marilyn on location with Paula Strasberg. Most of Marilyn's directors had been angered by Paula's interference on set, but Wilder firmly established who was boss early on.

Problems on set

Left: During the shooting of the bathing scene, Marilyn wore a 1920s swimsuit that was considerably more modest than most of the swimsuits she had been photographed in previously. On the first attempt at shooting this scene, a shark was believed to have been spotted in the water, so filming had to be stopped three hours earlier than planned.

Opposite: Director Billy Wilder gives Marilyn some quiet advice. When Joe Hyams of the *New York Herald* interviewed Wilder toward the end of filming, he complained of Marilyn's unpunctuality and inability to remember lines. When asked if he would work with her again, he replied, "I have discussed this with my doctor and my psychiatrist and they tell me I'm too old and too rich to go through this again." However, this was the reaction of the moment and he later said of Marilyn, "Anyone can remember lines, but it takes a real artist to come on the set and not know her lines and yet give the performance she did!"

On the beach

Above: Marilyn and Billy Wilder on the beach during the filming of *Some Like It Hot*.

Opposite: Tony Curtis posing as bogus oil baron Mr Shell to attract Sugar's attention. Although set in Florida, the exterior scenes were filmed at the Hotel del Coronado, a Victorian mansion built in the 1880s near San Diego which had been a haunt of the rich and famous over the years and was said to have been where Edward VIII met Mrs Simpson.

A great success

Above: Sugar chats to Josephine, while she takes her bath. Tony Curtis became terribly frustrated at Marilyn's inability to remember her lines, which often led to dozens of takes of simple scenes, and at her habitual lateness. At times Marilyn seemed unable to cope with even the simplest dialogues needing more than 40 takes to say "It's me, Sugar." Curtis famously commented to journalists that kissing Marilyn was "like kissing Hitler," but he later said that it was a throwaway line that had been taken far too seriously. Although Marilyn was upset she always refused to fight her battles in the press, and merely replied that Curtis had only said it because she wore prettier dresses in the movie. Despite all the problems during production, and even a disastrous preview, *Some Like It Hot* was a huge success at the box office, becoming one of the three top-earning pictures of 1959. It has become a classic movie, still entertaining audiences 40 years later, and is counted amongst Marilyn's best-ever performances.

Opposite: Frenchman Maurice Chevalier admires Marilyn's assets as he tours the set of *Some Like It Hot*. Marilyn's rather revealing dress had been designed by Orry-Kelly who created it specifically for the picture. The movie received six Oscar nominations, including Jack Lemmon for Best Actor, and Wilder for Best Director, but Orry-Kelly, nominated for Best Costume Design, was the only winner.

In the public eye

Opposite: Arthur Miller and Marilyn attending the première of *Some Like It Hot* at Loew's Capitol Theater on Broadway in New York, on March 29, 1959. Marilyn had lost her baby early the previous December, and had been staying out of the public eye as she recuperated.

Above: Arthur Miller tries to shoo away photographers at the Boston Arts Center Theater, close to Miller's home at Roxbury, Connecticut, where they had come to see a performance of *Macbeth*. Miller found the constant attention of the press and public difficult to bear.

Right: Marilyn poses on arrival in Los Angeles.

Running wild

Opposite: A candid shot of Marilyn, taken on the beach. Her hair had been lightened to almost white for *Some Like It Hot* and it was beginning to show the strain of all those years of bleaching.

Left: Writer Carson McCullers greets Marilyn with a kiss. The two women had known each other since Marilyn's early days in New York in 1955 when she and Marilyn had both been occupants of the Gladstone Hotel on East 52nd Street.

Below: Marilyn meets Danish author Isak Dinesen—otherwise known as Baroness Karen Blixen, author of *Out of Africa*—at the New York home of Carson McCullers. Both she and Arthur Miller had been invited to the event, which took place during Blixen's lecture tour of America in February 1959.

Smiling despite adversity

Opposite and above: Arthur Miller escorts Marilyn away from Lennox Hill Hospital, where she had been having corrective surgery to try to cure her chronic endometriosis. Despite appearances, their marriage was already in deep trouble as Marilyn had become convinced that her failure to give him a child would drive him away.

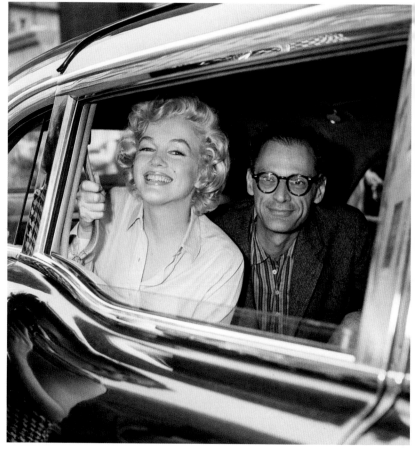

Back to work

Above: Arthur Miller and Marilyn leave hospital. She was due to begin work on *The Billionaire*, later called *Let's Make Love*, but in the event did not start on the project until early in 1960. The leading man was to have been Gregory Peck, but by the start of filming he had moved to another project and there were many problems in finding someone to replace him. Miller had spent months working on revisions to his screenplay for *The Misfits* and hoped that Marilyn would be free to begin shooting the movie in April 1960.

Opposite: Marilyn braves icy winds a as she arrives in Chicago for the release there of *Some Like It Hot*.

Meeting Khrushchev

Above: Marilyn and Arthur in November 1959.

Right: Marilyn strikes a pensive pose as she listens to Nikita Krushchev speak. Marilyn had always been interested in Russia—all her drama coaches had based their teaching on the work of Russian actor and director Konstantin Stanislavsky. When Soviet leader Nikita Khrushchev visited the Fox studios during his tour of America, she flew from New York to attend the lunch in his honor and for once in her life arrived early.

Opposite: Despite looking luminously beautiful in this publicity picture, by the end of 1959, Marilyn was in a poor state of health, and the start of filming on *Let's Make Love* was delayed as she regularly called in sick. This was not unusual on occasion, but now there were days on end when she did not arrive for work. Apart from her problems with prescription drugs and alcohol, this was also her way of showing that she was not happy with the script, and Arthur Miller was called in to rewrite whole sections of it. His involvement was never credited, as the forthcoming *The Misfits* was to be billed as both his screenwriting debut and the first time he had written anything specifically for Marilyn.

CHAPTER SIX

The Misfits

The plot of *Let's Make Love* is a comedy of mistaken identity and misunderstanding. It involves a show in production in Greenwich Village that is a satirical life history of fictional billionaire Jean-Marc Clément. The billionaire himself hears about the production, turns up at rehearsal, and falls for blonde bombshell Amanda Dell. The director mistakes him for a look-alike come to audition for the part of Jean-Marc Clément in the show—and because of his amazing resemblance he gets the part… Originally, much of the comedy depended on the fact that Jean-Marc Clément was not able to sing or dance, but was required to do so to appear in the show and get the girl—which was why Gregory Peck had originally been cast. After he dropped out, several other stars turned the part down but Miller suggested Yves Montand, who was in the United States touring with his one-man show. His English was poor and he was a renowned song-and-dance man, which were contrary to the demands of the plot. These drawbacks were instantly overlooked when he agreed to do the movie, because Fox were desperate to get it underway before they lost any more time. Marilyn, Miller, Montand, and his wife, Simone Signoret, soon became great friends, sharing adjacent bungalows at the Beverly Hills Hotel. Marilyn went shopping with Simone, Miller coached Montand with his English. That didn't stop Montand and Marilyn starting a passionate affair after Miller left for New York to work on the script of *The Misfits*, and Signoret returned to France.

Opposite: Marilyn in *Let's Make Love*.

For Marilyn, the affair was not so much about falling in love as seeking attention and some much-needed affection. Miller had abandoned her again to work on his script, and although *The Misfits* was supposed to be for her, she now firmly believed it was really all about getting his own career back on track. Perhaps Marilyn also began her affair because she wanted to see how Miller would react—would he still care, would he be angry and upset and come running? The answer was no. Grateful that at last Marilyn seemed happy to be working, he decided to leave well alone. As for Montand, he was a stranger in Hollywood and was enticed into an affair with a beautiful woman, far from home. He didn't expect it to lead anywhere—and for that matter neither did Marilyn. Signoret also ignored what was going on—when asked about it later she replied that if Marilyn was in love with her husband it just proved what good taste she had.

Apart from this, the filming of *Let's Make Love* proceeded predictably, with the usual lateness on set, forgotten lines, and missed calls. The major difference from director George Cukor's point of view was that he did not have to deal with Paula Strasberg, Marilyn having fallen out with her.

Meanwhile, Miller had virtually completed the script of *The Misfits*, which was due to begin filming in July. From the beginning he had an ambiguous and unresolved attitude to the whole project. On the one hand, he was creating a vehicle for Marilyn, and his personal life with her meant that there were themes he could not bring himself to explore. On the other, he was continually striving to repeat the success of *Death of a Salesman*, and hoped that *The Misfits* would prove to be as good, if not better. A further complication was that he took a stance of moral superiority over Hollywood—referring to Marilyn's loyal audience as "the great unwashed"—even while he was trying to tap into the success and riches of the movie business himself. He had partly resolved this to himself by hoping that *The Misfits* would not go on general release, but would be roadshowed in select cinemas, with exclusive and expensive showings. Director John Huston quickly disabused him of this idea—it was apparent to him that what Miller had created was a potentially good and workable movie, but not a masterpiece.

Because *Let's Make Love* had run so late—not solely due to Marilyn but also because of an actors' strike—she had to go almost straight from one project to the other. Given the emotional demands that working made on her, this was always going to be dangerous because she had no time to build up her reserves again. The other problem was the nature of the material. Marilyn had hoped and believed that Miller would create an exciting and different dramatic role for her to play, but instead all he had come up with was just another version of Marilyn. He gave his character, Roslyn, feelings that Marilyn had, put words into her mouth that Marilyn had spoken, made her act just like Marilyn. When he had started he had been in love with Marilyn, so his Roslyn was in many ways an idealized and sanitized version of her. Now the Millers were almost on the point of divorce, held together only by the project, and he had a very different view of his wife. Unfortunately, he had been unable to translate this effectively into the role, so Roslyn was not a rounded person. Marilyn was devastated that he had chosen to portray her as so vulnerable, wounded and helpless, with no depth or complexity and so little to offer. It made her uncomfortable that he both refused to acknowledge her dark side, and that he had revealed so many private moments of her life for all to see on screen.

There were even more tensions and fights than usual during filming—all exacerbated by the fact that they were working in the Nevada desert in July, with daytime temperatures often over 100ºF. Halfway through filming, Marilyn's health completely broke down, and she left Nevada for Los Angeles, where she checked into the Westside Hospital for ten days. However, she returned to complete the movie, which finished shooting a month later. Not long afterward, Marilyn and Miller announced that they had separated, and a couple of days later, her co-star Clark Gable died of a heart attack. The film has become so famous for these events, and for the problems on set, that its quality is often overlooked. Gable gave one of his finest performances, and despite everything Marilyn is superb.

The forthcoming divorce from Miller meant yet another failure for Marilyn, who was still recovering from doing the two movies back-to-back and trying to function despite her increasing dependence on drugs. She went back to New York, hoping to find sanctuary with the Strasbergs, but instead of allowing her to rest, Strasberg talked her into agreeing to appear in Somerset Maugham's *Rain*, which he planned to direct. He felt that completing a serious acting role successfully would restore her self-esteem, but he also had no previous movie credits, so he needed Marilyn to get the project off the ground.

On Christmas Eve 1960, Marilyn was alone, but suddenly a mass of flowers was delivered. The card with them said, "Best, Joe." As Marilyn said to her assistant, there was only one Joe, and from that moment he began to feature once again in her life.

Marilyn traveled to Mexico to file for divorce on 20 January 20, 1961, in the hopes that the inauguration of President John F. Kennedy on the same day would keep the press occupied. A few days later she attended the preview of *The Misfits*, but she and Miller carefully avoided each other. She became even more deeply depressed afterward, and on the advice of her analyst, Dr Kris, she signed herself into the Payne-Whitney Clinic under the name Faye Miller. In the state she was in, Marilyn probably did not realize that the Payne-Whitney was a psychiatric hospital. She had always been terrified of going mad and being locked away, because she believed her family had a history of insanity. Her great-grandfather had committed suicide, her grandfather had died in hospital suffering from dementia, and her grandmother, Della, had been diagnosed as a manic-depressive. In addition, her mother, Gladys, had spent years going in and out of various hospitals. However, the facts may not be quite so straightforward. Her great-grandfather had killed himself when his health was failing and his farm was about to be repossessed—and many people committed suicide during the Great Depression of the 1930s. Her grandfather had suffered dementia, but later study of his medical records seemed to show it was almost certainly caused by an infection that attacked his brain tissue—and not by an inherited weakness. Her grandmother, Della, died of heart disease and had also suffered a stroke, both of which can lead to erratic behavior, and there is no real evidence that she was psychotic. As for Gladys, she certainly suffered from depression, but at the time the illness was often not properly diagnosed, while the effects of new drugs were not fully understood. Several of her friends believed that a temporary inability to cope became a lifelong incapacity, purely because of the effect of the drugs she was prescribed.

However, when Marilyn realized where she was, she apparently broke a glass door with a chair and threatened to cut herself if she was not immediately released. Attendants subdued her, and carried her to the ward for violent patients, where she was sedated and restrained. She tried to contact the Strasbergs, but it was DiMaggio who finally found her and obtained her release. Although doctors initially said she was not fit to leave, he insisted that she was transferred and took her to the Columbia-Presbyterian Medical Center—another hospital, but at least not a psychiatric one.

Despite all this, Strasberg was still trying to get *Rain* off the ground, and Fox were pushing her to make a comedy movie called *Goodbye, Charlie* as the last picture they were owed under her contract. No one seemed to realize that it was largely the way she worked that had put her in hospital in the first place. In the event, Cukor, the approved director for *Goodbye, Charlie*, dropped out of the project and none of the other directors named in her contract could do it—except Lee Strasberg. He suddenly ceased to object to Marilyn making another comedy when

he saw the chance to command a fee as her director. In the event, the fee he wanted was too large, and Fox agreed to forgo the project as long as Marilyn agreed that they were still owed a movie. Strasberg's own project, *Rain*, also fell through and Marilyn refused to make it without him.

After Marilyn had left the hospital, DiMaggio had taken her off to Florida, where he was working with the Yankees during their spring training. There she sat in the sun, walked on the beach and generally enjoyed DiMaggio's company—although they were now just friends and there was no possibility of a new marriage. It was not the end of her health problems—she was admitted to hospital twice more that year: for an operation to correct an unspecified internal problem, and for surgery to remove her gallbladder.

Back in Hollywood in the summer of 1961, Marilyn was soon involved in the world of endless parties and entertaining, and it was inevitable that she would be invited to Peter Lawford's beach house. She already knew Lawford from her early days in Hollywood, and he was a friend of Sinatra, but Lawford's parties were now the ones to be invited to because he was married to Pat Kennedy. Sooner or later his brothers-in-law, the President and the Attorney-General, would be attending. It was at Lawford's house that Marilyn met both Kennedy brothers, and although she may have had a fling with the President, it was Bobby Kennedy with whom she started a more serious affair.

The dream of a new life in New York was now well and truly over, so Marilyn decided to base herself back in Hollywood, although she still kept her Manhattan apartment. She found a small apartment on Doheny Drive, in the same house in which she had lived when she first became a star nearly seven years earlier. It may have seemed like coming home, but perhaps it was just an attempt to pretend that the last few years had not happened.

Let's Make Love

Director George Cukor
discusses a scene with
Marilyn. Choreographer Jack
Cole had worked out the
dance sequences for *Let's
Make Love*. Cole had worked
on all Marilyn's dance routines
since *Gentlemen Prefer Blondes*
in 1953. She trusted him
implicitly and had specifically
requested his services
for *Let's Make Love*. Cukor,
exasperated at having to
deal with Marilyn's constant
lateness and insecurities, left
much of the direction of the
dance scenes to Cole. Marilyn
and Cole were firm friends,
but working on this project
strained their relationship to
the limit. Marilyn's marriage to
Arthur Miller was unraveling
fast, and her intake of pills
was rising rapidly. Studio
executives were also alarmed
that she didn't look as good
on camera as usual–the
daily rushes were often
disappointing. Despite
all her problems, she had
always managed to produce
something magical for the
camera—but this time it was
not to be.

Welcome to Hollywood!

On January 15, 1960, Twentieth Century Fox hosted a cocktail party in Hollywood to welcome Yves Montand—who was to co-star in *Let's Make Love* with Marilyn. He was not the first choice—Gregory Peck had originally been slated for the part, but had to drop out after delays in filming meant the dates would clash with other commitments. Several other well-known actors, including Cary Grant and Jimmy Stewart, had turned the part down, before Arthur Miller suggested Montand.

Part of the reason for the party was also to introduce the cast to the press. Montand was not well known in America—and his English was far from fluent—but his recent one-man shows in Los Angeles and New York had been a great success. Right from the start there was a certain chemistry between Marilyn and Montand—and it was not long before they started a passionate love affair. At the time, Miller was working on rewrites of the script of *Let's Make Love* and was desperate to finish the movie so Marilyn could move on to his project, *The Misfits*.

A growing friendship

Left and above: Monroe and Montand at the studio cocktail party. Arthur Miller and Yves Montand became great friends even before filming started—Montand had appeared in the French production of Miller's play, *The Crucible*. Montand's wife, Simone Signoret, and Marilyn also got on very well. At the start of filming *Let's Make Love* the two couples rented adjacent bungalows at the Beverly Hills Hotel and spent a great deal of time together. However, in April 1960 Miller returned to New York, leaving Marilyn to finish work on the movie, while Simone Signoret had already returned to France. It was almost inevitable that Marilyn and Montand, left alone together, would begin a relationship.

Opposite: Marilyn and Yves Montand rehearse on set. Marilyn told reporters that next to her husband and Marlon Brando, Montand was the most attractive man she knew. What she did not mention was that she had told friends in private that he reminded her of Joe DiMaggio.

Rehearsing with Jack Cole

Marilyn rehearses a dance routine
for the movie *Let's Make Love*
with choreographer Jack Cole.
The scene was a rehearsal within
a rehearsal, as the film was set
backstage as a theater company
puts together a satirical play with
song and dance routines. She
performed several of her routines
with accomplished song-and-
dance man Frankie Vaughan.

Too many curves?

Opposite: Marilyn with Yves Montand. At the start of filming Marilyn was quite svelte, but during the enforced halt caused by the actors' and writers' strike during March 1960 she put on a considerable amount of weight and in some later scenes she looks distinctly chubby. Cukor complained that this meant it took much longer to set up each scene as he had to film Marilyn from the most flattering angle.

Above: Yves Montand and Marilyn at the piano. Montand and Frankie Vaughan were not the only song-and-dance men to have roles in the movie. Gene Kelly and Bing Crosby also made cameo appearances in the movie.

Left: Marilyn pictured during rehearsals.

My Heart Belongs to Daddy...

Studio head Buddy Adler complained that Marilyn looked so overweight in the first version of this dance sequence that it seemed as if she was pregnant. He also hated the chalky-white makeup that had been developed for her role, similar to that used in *Bus Stop*. In *Bus Stop* it had been appropriate, as her character of Cherie worked nights and slept through the day, but now it made her look even more unhealthy. Producer Jerry Wald tried to assure him that the dance sequence would be so fast-paced in the final edit that the audience would not notice Marilyn's looks.

However, delays in filming had caused the movie to be $500,000 over budget, and despite all their concerns about Marilyn's appearance, there were to be no retakes.

Sewn in

Above: Adler also explained that a major reason for the "bumpy" look round Marilyn's middle was that the sweater she was wearing had been sewn to her leotard, causing it to move strangely and ride up. He claimed that if the stitching was removed, the sweater would move loosely and naturally and the problem would be solved. Marilyn had been working on set on her own, filming all the song and dance sequences, and she had yet to complete the bulk of her scenes with Montand, even though the proposed start date for *The Misfits* was now looming.

Take it from the top...

Right: Marilyn in pensive mood on the set of *Let's Make Love*. However bad she was feeling, Marilyn could usually raise a smile for the camera. Since early January 1960, she had been seeing a new psychoanalyst, Dr Ralph Greenson, who had been recommended by her analyst in New York. Greenson tried to limit her intake of pills and to help her regain some kind of composure so she could complete the movie. He was to remain her analyst until her death, some two years later.

Below: A still from the finished scene, in which Marilyn dances and sings Cole Porter's "My Heart Belongs to Daddy."

Celebration!

Opposite: Twentieth Century Fox studio head Buddy Adler welcomes Marilyn as she arrives to complete *Let's Make Love*.

Left: Marilyn proudly displays her Golden Globe award, which had just been presented by members of the Hollywood Foreign Press Association for her performance as the "Best Actress in a Motion Picture Comedy" in *Some Like It Hot*. Many were surprised that she had not also been nominated for a "Best Actress" award at that year's Oscars but Marilyn warmly congratulated Simone Signoret, who had been nominated for her role in *Room at the Top*.

Flying down to Reno

Right: Gail Sawyer, daughter of Nevada Governor Grant Sawyer, presents Marilyn with a bouquet of roses as she arrives at Reno Airport to begin work on *The Misfits*. Miller had embarked on writing the script for Marilyn as a way of showing his love for her, but as the relationship disintegrated she viewed it less as a gift of love and more as him using her name to get his first screenplay off the ground.

The Misfits

Left: Marilyn poses with some of the cast and crew of *The Misfits*. At the top of the picture is Arthur Miller, with Eli Wallach below him, and at the front are Montgomery Clift, Marilyn, and Clark Gable. Director John Huston is standing behind Marilyn. Marilyn poses with her usual carefree smile intact—despite the fact that Montand had now returned to France and his wife, so her very public affair with him was over.

Below: A scene from *The Misfits*, in which Gay (Clark Gable) and Roslyn (Marilyn) plant lettuces.

Opposite: Marilyn played Roslyn Tabor, in Reno to get a divorce from her husband. She drives a seriously dented car, as men are always driving into her to get an introduction. Marilyn felt the character of Roslyn was too sweet and saccharine to be at all believable.

Writing the script

Director John Huston, Marilyn and Arthur Miller confer on set. All the way through shooting Miller was rewriting and adjusting the script and was still unable to decide how the piece would end. Although Huston had at first said it was "magnificent," he still felt it needed serious cuts and revisions. Miller hoped he had written a great American story, something to rival his most successful play, *Death of a Salesman*, but Huston was more realistic and could see that the story was deeply flawed. Miller believed in his creation so much that he was unable to step back and reappraise it. Marilyn was hurt and angry that Roslyn, who was so obviously based on herself, revealed no elements of her own dark side. She felt this was due to Miller's inability to accept this aspect of her life—and took it as a rejection of the person she really was.

A not so happy couple

Above: Arthur Miller and Marilyn on the set of *The Misfits* in 1960, as filming is coming to an end. Although they still kept up the pretence of being together in public, it is noticeable that in these pictures Marilyn does not have her usual bright smile or sparkle, and that there seems to be a certain distance between husband and wife. By the time shooting was nearly over there were rumors that Miller was having an affair with Inge Morath, a young photographer who was visiting the set, and Marilyn had moved into Paula Strasberg's suite at the hotel. Only a week after the movie wrapped they announced their plans to divorce.

Opposite: Gable gives Marilyn a big hug. Despite the heat and the strain of waiting for Marilyn, he did not turn against her. When he died of a heart attack soon after shooting finished, many people blamed her behavior for causing him stress, but it was more likely his insistence on doing some of his own stunts or the fact that he was a heavy smoker that had led to the problems with his heart. On set Gable was calm and patient with both Marilyn and Montgomery Clift who was also a troubled personality. However, Marilyn said of Clift that he was "the only person I know who's in worse shape than me."

At a low ebb

Right: Marilyn's relationship with Arthur Miller was not her only problem. While making *The Misfits* her health had deteriorated to such a state that she had to be hospitalized for several days. Her dependence on prescription drugs had made it almost impossible for her to work and by the time filming was over Marilyn was at a very low ebb.

Opposite: Marilyn poses in one of the wigs made for her to wear in the movie.

Below: Marilyn arrives at Capitol Theater on Broadway on January 31, 1961, for a preview of *The Misfits*. Miller was also there with his children, but the two of them avoided each other. A typical review from the *New York Daily News* said, "Miss Monroe has seldom looked worse; the camera is unfailingly unflattering. But there is a delicacy about her playing and a tenderness that is affecting."

In and out of hospital

Left and opposite: Marilyn leaves the Columbia-Presbyterian Medical Center, where she had spent three weeks trying to pull herself out of the depths of depression.

Above: Joe DiMaggio, who was in Florida helping to coach the New York Yankees during their spring training session, invited Marilyn to join him there to recuperate after her release from the Columbia-Presbyterian Hospital, where she had undergone an operation to have her gallbladder removed. It was the fifth time she had been admitted to hospital in ten months.

Something's Got To Give

At the beginning of 1962, Marilyn was seeing her analyst, Dr Ralph Greenson, every day. There are mixed views about his treatment of Marilyn. On the one hand, he was undoubtedly totally committed to her, but on the other, many believe that he became far too emotionally involved and had lost any semblance of objective distance. Even more controversially, he involved Marilyn in his home life–as he did to an extent some other patients—and she often had dinner there after her sessions, sometimes stayed overnight and had even spent her last Christmas with his family. One of the first rules of psychoanalysis is that the analyst should avoid personal involvement, but Greenson appeared to believe that traditional methods had failed with Marilyn, and that what she actually needed was to experience a normal, stable family life. His detractors accuse him of wanting to control Marilyn—as many men had tried to do before—and he certainly attempted to screen who she saw. His friend, Eunice Murray, became her housekeeper, and it was Murray who found the house on Fifth Helena Drive that became Marilyn's last home. Marilyn liked it because it was a Mexican-style building that was reminiscent of Greenson's house.

Excited about having a proper home of her own, Marilyn planned to fly to Mexico to buy furniture, artwork, and tiles so she could create the same kind of colorful Mexican décor that she had enjoyed at the Greenson house. By all accounts she hoped the move would mark yet another new beginning, and in an effort to tie up loose ends, she had agreed to do *Something's Got To Give* for Fox, to complete her studio commitment. Unfortunately, in the midst of this positive atmosphere, word came that Miller was to marry again. The news affected Marilyn badly—it brought back all her lost dreams of being a good wife, having a family and creating a home. When she came back from Mexico, she had obviously slipped back into the old cycle of too many pills, mixed with too much champagne.

A few days after her return, Marilyn arrived at the Golden Globe Awards, obviously the worse for drink. When she collected her statuette for World's Favorite Female Star, her acceptance speech was rambling and inconclusive and gossip started in Hollywood that she was finished. Despite this, a couple of weeks later Marilyn had pulled herself together enough to report for costume fitting and makeup tests for her new movie, and the studio breathed a sigh of relief.

The plot of *Something's Got To Give* was based on *My Favorite Wife*, a popular 1940 comedy about a woman who has been shipwrecked on a desert island for many years and is believed dead, but who finally returns home to find her husband is married to another woman. The original script needed work and Marilyn was delighted when Fox appointed Nunnally Johnson to rewrite it. Johnson had written the screenplay for *How to Marry a Millionaire*, and although Marilyn had spent years trying to get away from the kind of dumb blonde character he had created, she

Opposite: A publicity shot for *Something's Got To Give*.

now knew she desperately needed a big hit to boost her reputation and silence wagging tongues. Anyway, the role of Ellen Arden would be different, because for the first time she would be playing a wife and mother. Another inducement was her co-star, Dean Martin, and Fox had also appointed Cukor to direct, with whom Marilyn had worked on *Let's Make Love*.

Johnson created a script that Marilyn was pleased with, and which incorporated many of her ideas, but he left the project before filming began. A series of other scriptwriters then worked on it and Marilyn became increasingly unhappy as the screenplay moved away from Johnson's version. New pages were always sent out to cast and crew on different-colored paper, so that everyone could be sure they were working from the same sheet, but at one point the studio resorted to sending rewritten pages on white paper to Marilyn, to try to fool her that no changes were being made.

Because of the script problems, shooting was put back until April 23, but by then Marilyn was ill and Dean Martin also failed to appear as he was still working on another movie. Although Marilyn managed several days' work over the next few weeks, she spent much more time at home with a fever–although she continued to work there with Paula Strasberg, trying to make some sense of the rewrites that continued to arrive daily. She now often went to see Greenson twice a day.

In the middle of all this, Greenson and his wife left for a long-planned trip to Europe. Greenson said later that he had become worried about Marilyn's increasing dependence on him, and that he himself desperately needed a break from the pressures of dealing with her. The week after he left, Marilyn turned up at the studio early and worked hard each day. She had been invited to sing "Happy Birthday" to the President at a gala 45th birthday salute at Madison Square Garden and she was desperate to go. The previous week, there had been a great deal of publicity about the fact that Miller had been an honored guest at a presidential dinner party for the French Minister of Culture, and Marilyn was determined not to miss the chance to show that she was a presidential favorite

too. Nevertheless, the studio was reluctant to let her go, because filming of *Something's Got To Give* was running so far behind.

On Thursday May 17, Marilyn worked until noon, then flew to New York to prepare for Saturday night. She came on as the finale, singing the simple song in an outrageously sexy way that delighted the entire audience. By Sunday evening she was on her way back to Los Angeles, ready to start work again on Monday morning, and she continued to report for filming the following week. As far as she was concerned she had only missed one day, and that was that. The studio executives at Fox saw it differently. At the time the entire movie industry was going through upheaval, and the old guard at Fox were being criticized for indulging the stars and giving in to their whims at the expense of the stockholders. In Italy *Cleopatra* was being filmed with Elizabeth Taylor and Richard Burton, and although it had already cost millions it was still going over budget; Fox had been forced to sell off part of its back lot to pay for it all. It was the wrong moment for Marilyn to challenge the studio's authority.

Behind the scenes, there was already talk of either closing the movie down or firing Marilyn and replacing her with someone else. Whether or not she was aware of these rumors, Marilyn continued to work intermittently, and relations with Cukor deteriorated. On June 1, she celebrated her thirty-sixth birthday with the cast and crew, and maybe the thought of getting older affected her badly, as it was the last day she appeared on set. The following week, desperate negotiations went on between her agent and Fox, in conjunction with Greenson—who had been hastily called back from his trip. Despite assurances that Marilyn would be back at work after a week's rest, Fox fired her from the movie. They had intended to replace her with Lee Remick, but Dean Martin refused to hear of it, saying he had signed to co-star with Marilyn and if she wasn't part of the deal, then neither was he. For the moment the picture was put on hold, while everyone considered their options.

In Marilyn's camp, they knew they needed some good publicity, and fast, to counteract the rumors that she had finally had a complete breakdown. Just before the movie closed down, Marilyn had done a photo session on set in which she swam in a pool, and had mischievously removed her costume under water. The resulting nudes were sensational, and they were quickly released—one appeared on the cover of *Life* magazine at the end of the month. Another high-profile photography session was organized with Bert Stern, for *Vogue*. The publicity and the groundswell of public opinion, which was sympathetic to Marilyn, did make Fox think again. By mid-July Marilyn was informed that they had agreed in principle to reinstate her, although final details of the deal were still being worked out and filming could not begin again until early September because Dean Martin was fulfilling other commitments.

It seemed as if, once again, Marilyn would manage to turn disaster into triumph, but in reality those close to her were worried about whether she was currently capable of working. Unlike previous times when she had been down and apparently out, but had come back fighting, this time she seemed to be finding it more difficult.

On August 3, Marilyn persuaded Dr Engelberg to give her a prescription for twenty-five Nembutal tablets. Engelberg and Greenson had been working together to control her drug intake, but for some reason they did not communicate about this prescription. The following day, Greenson came to Marilyn's house and spent much of the afternoon with her. She had been invited to dinner at Lawford's house, and Greenson was also going out to dinner so he left around 7.00 pm. Nearly an hour later, Lawford called to find out if Marilyn was coming over, and was concerned at her slurred speech. When Marilyn finished the call by telling him goodbye, alarm bells rang and he in turn telephoned Marilyn's lawyer, Milton Rudin, who called her housekeeper. Eunice Murray assured him that Marilyn was fine. It was not until the early hours of August 5 that Murray became concerned that the light was still on in Marilyn's room. Everyone knew she was unable to sleep if there was the slightest chink of light in the room, and her bedroom was always fitted with blackout drapes. Murray called Greenson, and the two of them broke into the room, to find Marilyn sprawled across the bed, the telephone receiver still in her hand. She had been dead for some time, and an autopsy showed large amounts of both Nembutal and chloral hydrate in her system.

The theories about Marilyn's death could–and have–filled many books, and they range from a straightforward suicide to conspiracy and murder. The reality is that no one really knows the truth. She had certainly tried to commit suicide in the past, and she had also taken accidental overdoses. Given her lifestyle, it is also possible that additional medication was obtained from someone unaware of what she had already taken. However, it is highly unlikely that she was murdered, and none of the motives so far proposed hold water under close examination. The real tragedy is that previously she had always been found in time, and this time she wasn't.

Marilyn's funeral was held at Westwood Memorial Park, in Los Angeles, and was arranged by Joe DiMaggio with the help of her half-sister, Berniece Miracle, and her business manager, Inez Melson. DiMaggio refused to allow her Hollywood friends to attend, holding them morally responsible for her death, and press and photographers were kept at a distance. Her trusted makeup man, Whitey Snyder, did her makeup for her final appearance, fulfilling a promise made as a joke many years previously. DiMaggio also fulfilled an old promise, arranging for a single red rose to be delivered to her grave twice a week.

Even many years after her death, Marilyn Monroe is still one of the greatest legends of the twentieth century. In her movies she projected a unique and fascinating persona—a child-woman who was both innocent and full of sexuality, someone whom men desired, but who women found unthreatening. In real life, she was a beautiful and complex woman who felt deeply insecure, and who just wanted to be loved enough to wipe out her unhappy past. In her brief career she appeared in several classic movies, as well as many more that are memorable for her presence.

It was perhaps inevitable that Marilyn Monroe the person would die young, but Marilyn Monroe the star is an extraordinary and unforgettable woman whose legend still lives on.

Flying down to Mexico

Right: Joe gives Marilyn a goodbye kiss as she leaves for Mexico City on a short vacation in February 1962. She was traveling there to buy some Mexican-style furnishings for her newly acquired home in Hollywood. She had admired the style in the home of her analyst, Dr Ralph Greenson. Marilyn had not worked since shooting on *The Misfits* had finished towards the end of 1960, but the studio intended that she should begin filming *Something's Got To Give* as soon as rewrites to the script were complete.

Avoiding the camera

Opposite: But for the hair that has escaped from under the scarf, Marilyn almost succeeds in disguising herself as she uncharacteristically avoids the camera.

Left: Marilyn waves to newsmen on her return from Mexico City in March 1962. However, she was not in good spirits having heard that Arthur Miller had remarried.

Female World Film Favorite 1961

Opposite: In March 1962, Marilyn was presented with an award as Female World Film Favorite 1961 by the Foreign Press Association at their Annual Award ceremony in Hollywood. Actor Rock Hudson presented the award to Marilyn, and seemed almost as pleased as she was. Her slim and glamorous new look belied the fact that she was both physically and mentally fragile.

Above: Marilyn arrives for the party after the ceremony with Mexican screenwriter José Bolaños. They had met during her recent trip to Mexico City, and after her death he told the world that they had planned to marry. However, the relationship didn't last for long.

Something's Got To Give

Left: Marilyn as Eve Arden in *Something's Got To Give*. Very little of it was completed before Marilyn was fired from the picture on June 8, 1962. The following year the script was revised yet again and the movie was made as *Move Over Darling*, with Doris Day in Marilyn's role, and James Garner taking the Dean Martin part.

Opposite above: On her 36th birthday, and on one of her last public appearances, Marilyn came onto the field at Chavez Ravine Dodger Stadium in Los Angeles, along with outfielder Albie Pearson, before a Yankees v Angels benefit game on June 1, 1962. She was appealing for donations to the Muscular Dystrophy fund.

Skinny-dipping

Left: During a swimming scene in *Something's Got To Give*, when the press had been invited on set to take some pictures, Marilyn caused a sensation by removing her swimsuit underwater. Progress on the picture had been painfully slow at a time when the studio could ill afford to lose money and the atmosphere on set was tense. Although Marilyn looked superficially slimmer and fitter than she had done in several years, she was unable to function without medication and constant support from Dr Greenson, her psychoanalyst.

Day of the dead...

Above: After Marilyn was found dead, on August 5, 1962, the police were called to her home on Fifth Helena Drive. They searched unsuccessfully for a suicide note, and interviewed her analyst, Dr Ralph Greenson, Dr Engelberg, and housekeeper Eunice Murray. Reporters were prevented from approaching, but photographers look pictures of Marilyn's house with the two toy stuffed dogs on the lawn.

Left: The bedroom where Marilyn's body was found. She had still not really settled into the house, and much of the furniture and many of the decorative pieces she had ordered in Mexico had not yet been delivered. There were piles of bags in many corners, as there was no storage.

A quiet funeral

Above and left: Marilyn's funeral took place at the Westwood Funeral Chapel and was arranged by her old love, Joe DiMaggio. During the service she lay in an open casket, dressed in green. Her makeup man, Whitey Snyder, had done her makeup for the very last time—having been fortified by a large amount of gin. Joe had refused to allow her Hollywood friends to attend. So there were only thirty-one invited mourners including the Strasbergs, the Greenson family, and several of Marilyn's employees. Arthur Miller chose not to attend.

Grief stricken

Above: Joe DiMaggio, and his son Joe DiMaggio Jr—in his US Marine dress uniform—stand shoulder to shoulder at Marilyn's funeral. Joe Jr had been one of the last people to speak to Marilyn on the phone. A recent biography of DiMaggio claims that the day of the funeral—August 8, 1962—was to have been the day that he and Marilyn were to remarry. Since Marilyn's death much has been written about how she died. The autopsy report concluded that she had died of "acute barbiturate poisoning—ingestion of overdose." There were no signs of any external violence, but she had 8mg of chloral hydrate and 4.5mg of Nembutal in her bloodstream. The theories as to how this happened range from suicide, through accidental overdose to murder.

Opposite above: Marilyn's coffin bedecked with flowers at Westwood Park Chapel.

Opposite below: Marilyn's psychoanalyst, Dr Ralph Greenson, with his wife and two children, at the funeral.

Chronology

1926

Jun 1 Marilyn is born Norma Jeane Mortensen in Los Angeles, California

Jun 13 The new baby is left with the neighboring Bolender family after her mother returns to work

Dec At her christening, the baby is named Norma Jeane—but she spells her second name with and without the "e" throughout her childhood

1927

July The toddler Norma is nearly suffocated by her grandmother, Della Monroe, who is later admitted to the Metropolitan State Hospital in Norwalk, LA County

Aug 23 Della dies of a heart attack in hospital

1933

Jun Norma Jeane leaves the Bolenders to live with her mother, Gladys, in North Hollywood

Aug Gladys obtains a mortgage and they move into a house on Arbol Street, sharing it with an English couple

Oct Gladys hears that her grandfather, Tilford Hogan, has committed suicide

1934

Jan Gladys is admitted to a rest home in Santa Monica, having suffered a mental breakdown

1935

Jan Gladys is committed to the Metropolitan State Hospital in Norwalk, LA County, with a diagnosis of paranoid schizophrenia

Apr Gladys's estate is assessed as she is no longer able to manage her affairs

Jun 1 Grace McKee becomes responsible for liquidating Gladys's estate

Sept 13 Norma Jeane is placed in the Los Angeles Orphans Home Society

1936

Feb 26 Papers are filed to allow Grace McKee to become Norma Jeane's legal guardian

1937

Spring Grace becomes Norma Jeane's legal guardian

Jun 26 Norma Jeane leaves the orphanage and lives with Grace and her new husband

Nov Norma Jeane goes to live with Ida Martin, a distant relative in Compton, LA

1938

Aug Norma Jeane goes to live with Anna Lower, Grace's aunt

1941

Dec Norma Jeane begins dating Jim Dougherty

1942

Jun 19 Norma Jeane marries Jim Dougherty and the newlyweds move into an apartment

1943

Spring Jim and Norma Jeane move back to his parents' home, to look after it while they are away

Fall The young couple move into their own apartment again

Jim Dougherty is called up and joins the Merchant Marines—he is sent first as an instructor to Catalina Island

1944

Spring Jim is posted to a ship in the South Pacific

Apr Marilyn returns to her mother-in-law's home and starts work at Radio Plane Munitions Factory in Burbank, California

1945

Jun 26 At Radio Plane, Marilyn is photographed by David Conover for a feature in *Yank* magazine

Aug 2 Marilyn is taken on by the Blue Book Agency

1946

Apr 26 First appearance of Norma Jeane on the cover of a national magazine, *Family Circle*

Jun Norma Jeane dyes her brunette hair blonde

Jul Harry Lipton of National Concert Artists Corporation becomes Norma Jeane's agent

Jul 16 Norma Jeane has her first interview with Ben Lyon at Twentieth Century Fox

Jul 19 At a screen test for Twentieth Century Fox, Norma Jeane comes over very well

Jul 29 First mention of Norma Jeane (as Jean Norman) in a Hollywood gossip column

Aug 26 The aspiring actress signs her first studio contract, with Twentieth Century Fox, and changes her name to Marilyn Monroe

Sept While in Las Vegas to obtain her divorce, Norma Jeane spends time in Las Vegas General Hospital, first with an acute mouth infection after her wisdom teeth are removed, and then with measles

Sept 13 Norma Jeane is granted a divorce from Jim Dougherty in Las Vegas, Nevada

1947

Although Marilyn's first movie role is in *Scudda Hoo, Scudda Hay*, most of her part is later cut

Summer Filming of *Dangerous Years*, with Marilyn's first speaking role

Jul 26 Marilyn is told that her contract with Twentieth Century Fox is not to be renewed

Aug 25 Marilyn's contract with Twentieth Century Fox runs out

Dec 4 Marilyn signs a management contract with Lucille Ryman and John Carroll

Dec 7 Release of *Dangerous Years*

1948

Feb Marilyn meets Joe Schenck at a Hollywood party

Feb 20 Marilyn is crowned Miss California Artichoke Queen

Mar 9 Marilyn signs a six-month contract with Columbia

Vocal coach Fred Karger works with Marilyn on her songs for *Ladies of the Chorus*, but her devotion to him is not reciprocated

Apr Marilyn meets Natasha Lytess, head drama coach at Columbia, who later becomes her personal drama coach for some years

Filming of *Ladies of the Chorus*

Apr 14 *Scudda Hoo, Scudda Hay* is released

Sept 9 Marilyn's contract with Columbia is not renewed

Oct 22 Release of *Ladies of the Chorus*

Dec 31 Marilyn meets agent Johnny Hyde from the William Morris Agency at Sam Spiegel's New Year party

1949

Feb Marilyn films a part in *Love Happy*, and is mentioned in Louella Parsons' gossip column

May 27 Marilyn poses nude for the famous calendar photograph by Tom Kelley, which is published anonymously

Jul 24 Earl Wilson first interviews Marilyn

Aug 15 Start of shooting on *A Ticket to Tomahawk*

Johnny Hyde becomes Marilyn's agent

Marilyn films a small uncredited part in *Right Cross*

Oct MGM give Marilyn a contract for a role in *The Asphalt Jungle*

Oct 10 *Life* magazine shows pictures of Marilyn in a feature on Hollywood's aspiring stars

1950

Jan 5 Marilyn begins shooting *The Fireball*

Mar 27 Marilyn lands the part of a starlet in *All About Eve*

Apr 8 Release of *Love Happy*

May 11 Marilyn signs a new seven-year contract with Fox

May 19 Release of *A Ticket to Tomahawk*

May 23 World première of *The Asphalt Jungle* at Grauman's Egyptian Theater

Oct 14 Release of *All About Eve*

Nov 9 Release of *The Fireball*

Nov 15 Release of *Right Cross*

Dec 10 Marilyn signs a contract with Twentieth Century Fox

Dec 18 Johnny Hyde dies of a heart attack

Dec Marilyn has minor plastic surgery, possibly to remove a small lump from her nose

Dec Marilyn appears in *As Young As You Feel* for Fox

Dec Arthur Miller and Marilyn meet for the first time on the set of *As Young As You Feel* at Twentieth Century Fox

1951

Mar After catching the attention of Spyros Skouras, president of Fox, Marilyn secures the renewal of her contract

Mar 29 Marilyn is a presenter at the 1951 Academy Awards ceremony

Apr 18 Starts shooting *The Love Nest* for Fox

May 11 The six-month contract with Fox is converted to a seven-year contract

Release of *Hometown Story*

Films a part in *Let's Make it Legal* for Fox

Aug 2 Release of *As Young As You Feel*

Aug 21 Fox agrees to loan Marilyn to RKO, to appear in *Clash by Night*

Sept 8 The first full-length feature on Marilyn appears in *Colliers* magazine

Fall Marilyn tries to contact C. Stanley Gifford, the man she believed was her father, but he refuses to see her

Marilyn enrolls to study acting with coach Michael Chekov

Filming of *Clash by Night*

Filming of *Don't Bother to Knock*

Oct 10 Release of *Love Nest*

Oct 23 Marilyn appears on the cover of *Look* magazine for the first time

Nov 6 Release of *Let's Make It Legal*

Nov 15 *Quick* magazine has a feature on Marilyn as its cover story, designating her "The New Jean Harlow"

Dec *Focus* magazine has a cover story on Marilyn, comparing her favorably with Lana Turner, Betty Grable, and Rita Hayworth

1952

Feb 26 Marilyn begins filming *Monkey Business*

Mar 13 After the press discover Marilyn's nude calendar picture, she admits publicly that she is the model

Mar 15 Joe DiMaggio and Marilyn meet for the first time

Apr 7 Marilyn features on her first *Life* magazine cover

Apr 28 Marilyn's appendix is removed at the Cedars of Lebanon hospital

May 3 Studio publicity about Marilyn had presented her as an orphan, but after it is discovered that her mother is still alive, she releases a short statement to the press

Jun 1 Marilyn learns she has the part of Lorelei in *Gentlemen Prefer Blondes*

Jun Start of filming of *Niagara*

Jun 18 Release of *Clash by Night*

Jul 12 General release of *We're Not Married*

Jul 18 Release of *Don't Bother to Knock*

Aug New York première of *Don't Bother to Knock*

Aug 31 Marilyn's first live radio show is broadcast, in which she reads a role in a one-act play

Sept 1 The US Army photographs Marilyn to use in a recruitment drive, but the pictures are withdrawn after the photographer shoots from a balcony, revealing too much of the Monroe cleavage

Sept 2 At the Miss America beauty pageant, Marilyn is a Grand Marshal

Sept 5 General release of *Monkey Business*

Oct 16 Release of *O Henry's Full House*

Oct 26 Marilyn is heard on ventriloquist Edgar Bergen's radio show

Nov 17 Filming begins on *Gentlemen Prefer Blondes*

Nov 22 An article titled "The Truth about Me" appears in *The American Weekly*, with Marilyn's name as the by-line

1953

Jan The famous nude picture of Marilyn is republished as "Miss Golden Dreams" on the January page of a new calendar

Jan 21 *Niagara* is released

Feb 9 Gladys Baker is transferred to Rockhaven Sanatorium at Marilyn's expense

Mar 6 Filming on *Gentlemen Prefer Blondes* is completed

Mar 9 Scandal follows Marilyn's appearance at the *Photoplay* magazine awards in the tissue-thin gold lamé gown from *Gentlemen Prefer Blondes*

Mar *Photoplay* features an article by Jim Dougherty, "Marilyn Monroe Was My Wife"

Apr Start of filming on *How to Marry a Millionaire*

May Marilyn is featured on the cover of *Cosmopolitan* magazine

Jun 26 Marilyn and Jane Russell both leave their prints outside Grauman's Chinese Theater

Jul 15 Release of *Gentlemen Prefer Blondes*

Aug Filming of *River of No Return* in Canada

Aug 20 During filming, Marilyn slips and injures her leg

Aug Official première of *Gentlemen Prefer Blondes* at Grauman's Chinese Theater

Sept 13 Marilyn's first television appearance on *The Jack Benny Show*

Oct Marilyn signs a recording contract with RCA

Oct 10 Marilyn accompanies Joe DiMaggio to visit his family in San Francisco

Nov 4 Première of *How to Marry a Millionaire* in Los Angeles

Dec The famous nude calendar shot appears in the first issue of *Playboy* magazine, as the first Sweetheart of the Month, and a clothed Marilyn also appears on the cover

Dec 15 Marilyn fails to report on the first day of rehearsals of *The Girl in Pink Tights*

1954

Jan 4 Fox suspends Marilyn for failing to appear for filming

Jan 14 Marilyn marries baseball player Joe DiMaggio at San Francisco City Hall

Feb 2 The couple arrive in Tokyo for their honeymoon

Feb 16 During their honeymoon, Marilyn takes time to entertain the troops in Korea

Mar 5 Marilyn arrives back in Los Angeles

Mar 14 Marilyn is voted Best New Actress of 1953 by *Photoplay* magazine

Mar 31 Charles Feldman at Famous Artists Agency officially becomes Marilyn's agent

Apr 14 After the lifting of her suspension, Marilyn returns to the studio

Apr 30 Release of *River of No Return*

May 28 Starts filming *There's No Business Like Show Business*

Jul 7 A representative of the armed forces presents Marilyn with a trophy and plaque for morale-building activities

Aug 10 Filming begins on *The Seven Year Itch*

Sept 9 Marilyn arrives in New York for location filming on *The Seven Year Itch*

Sept 10 Milton Greene photographs Marilyn as a ballerina

Sept 16 The famous skirt-blowing sequence for *The Seven Year Itch* is filmed on the streets of New York

Oct 5 Marilyn and Joe DiMaggio officially separate

Oct 27 A divorce from DiMaggio is granted, but not finalized for one year

Nov 4 Shooting finishes on *The Seven Year Itch*

Nov 5 Joe DiMaggio and Frank Sinatra

carry out the "Wrong Door" raid, attempting to find Marilyn

Nov 6 Marilyn is honored at a Hollywood party at Romanoff's

Nov 7 Marilyn enters the Cedars of Lebanon Hospital to undergo surgery for endometriosis

Dec Leaving Hollywood, Marilyn heads for New York

Dec 16 Release of *There's No Business Like Show Business*

Dec 31 Marilyn Monroe Productions is officially formed

1955

Jan 7 Milton Greene and Marilyn hold a press conference to announce the creation of Marilyn Monroe Productions

Jan 10 Marilyn returns briefly to Hollywood to film one scene of additional dialogue for *The Seven Year Itch*

Jan 15 Fox suspends Marilyn again

Feb Marilyn begins to study under Lee Strasberg, founder of the Actors Studio in New York

Mar 9 At the première of *East of Eden*, Marilyn acts as an usherette in aid of the Actors Studio

Mar 30 At the opening of the Ringling Brothers' Barnum & Bailey Circus, Marilyn appears riding a pink elephant in aid of the New York Arthritis & Rheumatism Foundation

Apr 8 Edward R. Murrow interviews Marilyn live on *Person to Person*

Summer Marilyn briefly dates Marlon Brando, and when they split up they remain friends

Jun 1 World première of *The Seven Year Itch*

Jul 26 Breaking her agency contract with Famous Artists, Marilyn signs with MCA

Sept 29 Marilyn attends the opening night of Arthur Miller's play, *A View*

from the Bridge, at New York's Coronet Theater

Oct 31 The divorce from Joe DiMaggio is finalized

Dec 31 Marilyn signs a new four-picture, seven-year contract with Fox

1956

Jan 4 Twentieth Century Fox announce that they and Marilyn have come to terms, and that she will be returning to Hollywood

Feb 9 At a press conference in New York, Laurence Olivier announces their joint project, *The Prince and the Showgirl*

Feb 17 Marilyn performs at the Actors Studio, New York

Feb 23 Norma Jeane legally changes her name to Marilyn Monroe

Feb 25 Marilyn returns to Hollywood after her one-year exile in New York

Mar 3 Filming begins on *Bus Stop*

Apr 12 Suffering from bronchitis, Marilyn spends four days in St Vincent Hospital, Los Angeles

May 14 *Time* magazine features Marilyn on the cover for the first and only time in her lifetime

Jun 11 A divorce is granted to playwright Arthur Miller

Jun 29 Marilyn marries Miller in a civil ceremony

Jul 1 Marilyn and Miller have a Jewish wedding ceremony

Jul 14 The Millers fly to London

Aug 7 *The Prince and the Showgirl* starts filming in England

Aug 31 Release of *Bus Stop*

Sept Marilyn becomes pregnant, but loses the baby within a few weeks

Oct 29 Marilyn is presented to Queen Elizabeth II at the Royal Command Performance of *The Battle of the River Plate* in London

Nov 17 Filming completed on *The Prince and the Showgirl*

Nov 20 The Millers return to America

Dec 18 Marilyn does a radio show broadcast from the Waldorf-Astoria

1957

Feb 18 Miller is indicted by a federal grand jury on two counts of contempt of Congress

Feb 27 Frank Sinatra testifies at an investigation into the "Wrong Door" raid carried out by Joe DiMaggio in 1954

Mar 1 At a first hearing, Miller pleads not guilty

Apr 11 A statement is released, accusing Greene of mismanaging Marilyn Monroe Productions

May 14 After being called to Washington, Arthur Miller is put on trial for contempt of Congress; Marilyn accompanies him but stays out of sight

Jun 13 Première of *The Prince and the Showgirl*

Aug 1 Marilyn is rushed to Doctors Hospital, New York, with severe abdominal pain, which turns out to be an ectopic pregnancy that has to be terminated

Aug 10 Marilyn leaves hospital under a barrage of press attention

1958

Jan 28 Marilyn attends the annual March of Dimes fashion show at the Waldorf-Astoria, New York

Apr 4 After prevaricating, Marilyn signs the contract for *Some Like It Hot*

Jul 7 Marilyn returns to Hollywood to prepare for filming

Aug 4 Filming begins on *Some Like It Hot*

Oct Marilyn becomes pregnant again

Nov 6 Filming on *Some Like It Hot* is completed

Dec 16 Marilyn miscarries the baby, and is taken to Polyclinic Hospital in New York

1959

Mar 29 Première of *Some Like It Hot* at Loew's Capitol Theater on Broadway

Jun Marilyn receives the David Di Donatello statuette from Italy for her performance in *The Prince and the Showgirl*

Jun 23 Corrective gynecological surgery is carried out on Marilyn at the Lennox Hill Hospital, New York, to try to cure her chronic endometriosis

Sept 18 The Russian premier, Nikita Khrushchev, meets Marilyn at a luncheon in his honor at the Twentieth Century Fox studios in Hollywood

Oct 14 Although Marilyn is due to begin rehearsing in New York for *The Billionaire*—later released as *Let's Make Love*—she fails to show

Nov 9 Marilyn officially begins work on *Let's Make Love*

1960

Jan 25 The first part of one of Marilyn's musical numbers in *Let's Make Love* is finally filmed

Mar 8 Marilyn receives a Golden Globe award for Best Actress in a Comedy, for *Some Like It Hot*

Yves Montand and Marilyn have a brief affair during the filming of *Let's Make Love*

Jun Psychoanalyst Ralph Greenson begins seeing Marilyn on a daily basis

Jul 18 Filming begins on *The Misfits*

Aug 27 Marilyn is admitted to Westside Hospital in Los Angeles suffering from exhaustion

Sept 5 Marilyn returns to Nevada to finish location filming on *The Misfits*

Sept 8 Release of *Let's Make Love*

Nov 4 Shooting finishes on *The Misfits*

Nov Yves Montand sees Marilyn briefly in New York, before returning to his wife in France

Nov 11 Arthur Miller and Marilyn officially separate

Nov 16 Clark Gable dies of a heart attack

1961

Jan 20 A divorce from Arthur Miller is granted in Juarez, Mexico

Jan 31 Première of *The Misfits*

Feb 7 Marilyn enters the Payne-Whitney Clinic in New York under the name Faye Miller

Feb 11 After three days, Joe DiMaggio arranges for Marilyn to be transferred to the Neurological Institute at Columbia-Presbyterian Hospital

Mar 5 Marilyn leaves the Columbia-Presbyterian Hospital

Mar Margaret Parton interviews Marilyn for the *Ladies Home Journal*, but the interview is never published as it is deemed "too sympathetic" by the editor

May Again Marilyn enters the Cedars of Lebanon Hospital for a minor operation

Summer Frank Sinatra and Marilyn have a brief affair

Jun 28 Marilyn enters Polyclinic Hospital in New York to have her gallbladder removed

Jul 11 Marilyn leaves hospital

Aug 8 Finally giving up on New York, Marilyn returns to Hollywood

Oct Robert Kennedy and Marilyn begin an affair, after meeting at Peter Lawford's beach house

Nov 19 Marilyn attends a dinner at Peter Lawford's beach house; President John Kennedy is also present

1962

Feb Marilyn buys a new home in Brentwood, California

Feb 21 With her housekeeper, Marilyn flies to Mexico to buy furniture and artifacts for her new home

Mar 2 Marilyn returns from Mexico

Mar 5 At the Golden Globe Awards, Marilyn is presented with a statuette as the World's Favorite Female Star

Apr 10 Marilyn attends costume and makeup tests for *Something's Got To Give*

Apr 23 Filming begins on *Something's Got To Give*

May 19 Marilyn sings "Happy Birthday" at a gala birthday party for President John Kennedy at Madison Square Garden

May 28 During filming, Marilyn is photographed swimming nude in a pool

Jun 1 Marilyn's last public appearance

Jun 8 Marilyn is fired from *Something's Got To Give* for persistent absenteeism

Jun 23 First *Vogue* photo session with Bert Stein

Jun 28 Negotiations with Fox begin about resuming work on *Something's Got To Give*

Jun 29 Start of a three-day photo session, with George Barris shooting Marilyn for *Cosmopolitan*

Jul 4 Richard Meryman begins an extensive interview with Marilyn, which turns out to be her last

Jul 12 Marilyn meets the studio chiefs at Fox

Jul 20 Marilyn enters the Cedars of Lebanon Hospital for an operation to cure her endometriosis

Jul 28 Marilyn spends the weekend at Cal-Neva Lodge

Aug 1 Fox revises Marilyn's contract, offering double her previous salary and agreeing to restart shooting on *Something's Got To Give*

Aug 3 Marilyn appears on the cover of *Life* magazine for the last time before her death

Aug 4 Dr Ralph Greenson spends six hours with Marilyn

Aug 5 Police are called after Marilyn is found dead in her Brentwood home

Aug 8 Marilyn's funeral, at Westwood Memorial Park, in Los Angeles, California

1995

Jun 1 A 32¢ commemorative postage stamp featuring Marilyn is issued in the US Legends of Hollywood series

Oct Marilyn is voted UK's *Empire* magazine Sexiest Female Movie Star of All Time

1997

Oct Marilyn is listed No. 8 in the UK's *Empire* magazine The Top 100 Movie Stars of All Time

1998

Fall Marilyn is voted *Playboy* magazine's Sexiest Female Star of the Twentieth Century

1999

Oct At a Christie's auction of Marilyn memorabilia, the gown in which Marilyn sang "Happy Birthday" to John Kennedy is sold for over $1 million

Dec *Playboy* magazine names Marilyn as Number One Sex Star of the Twentieth Century

Bibliography

Marilyn Monroe   Barbara Leaming (Orion, London, 2002)

The Marilyn Encyclopedia   Adam Victor (The Overlook Press, New York, 2001)

Norma Jean   Fred Lawrence Guiles (Mayflower, St Albans, 1977)

My Story   Marilyn Monroe (Stein & Day, New York, 1974)

The Pocket Essential Marilyn Monroe   Paul Donnelley (Pocket Essentials, Harpenden, 2000)

Goddess, The Secret Lives of Marilyn Monroe   Anthony Summers (Gollanz, London, 1985)

DiMaggio Setting the Record Straight   Morris Engleberg, Marv Schneider (MBI, St Paul, 2003)

Blonde Heat   Richard Buskin (Billboard Books, New York, 2001)

The Assassination of Marilyn Monroe   Donald H. Wolfe (Time Warner Paperbacks, London 1998)

On Sunset Boulevard, The Life and Times of Billy Wilder   Ed Sikov (Hyperion, New York, 1998)

ACKNOWLEDGMENTS

The photographs in this book are reproduced by kind permission
of Corbis except those listed below.

*116, 146, 147, 148, 149 t, 150 br & bl, 151, 152/3, 154b, 155, 156, 157, 158, 159, 160/1,
162, 163, 164, 165, 253, which are courtesy of Associated Newspapers Archive.*

Every effort has been made to ensure that the copyright details shown are correct, but if
there are any inaccuracies, please contact the publisher.